WHEN
THE SMOKE CLEARS

Stories of Three Women

The Girl Who Wandered
The Woman Who Was Silent
The Woman Who Stood Tall

Robert J. McAllister, M.D.

authorHOUSE®

AuthorHouse™
1663 Liberty Drive
Bloomington, IN 47403
www.authorhouse.com
Phone: 1 (800) 839-8640

Published by AuthorHouse 08/29/2018

ISBN: 978-1-5462-5398-3 (sc)
ISBN: 978-1-5462-5397-6 (e)

Library of Congress Control Number: 2018909117

Print information available on the last page.

To:

The Woman Who Departed

ACKNOWLEDGEMENTS

My gratitude to all those who have helped with the shaping of my story and the preparation of its final form, especially my son (Paul), Elizabeth Beil, Ph.D., Rev. Joe Heim, Dennis Mauro-Huse and Sara Rubloff, LCSW-C.

Thanks to Casey and Ty McConville for cover work.

CONTENTS

THE GIRL WHO WANDERED

JAMES WATSON GREW UP ON A FARM EIGHT MILES OUT OF ELKO, NEVADA. His father, Jake, worked the farm for thirty years before Jim was born. Jim was the youngest of three children. His sister, Sara, was ten years older and his brother, Ted, was four years older. Jim didn't care for farm life. It was burdensome, too isolated and was "dirty work" in his mind. James' mother, Edna, was a quiet woman who kept busy with housework and her hobby of growing flowers. In Jim's estimation Sara was the family princess. She helped her mother with a smidgen of the housework but spent most of her time reading *literature* and visiting with friends in Elko. His brother became a sports-hero not only at school but in the town and notably in his father's eyes. His father was proud of Ted's "most valuable player" status.

Although Jim wasn't isolated from the family there was no evidence of attachment to any of them. After graduating from Elko High, he followed the course of his two siblings and went to the University of Nevada. He made friends with peers but was never close with anyone. In considering the future, the profession of law appealed to him. He saw law as a "win-lose" profession and an occupation in which a keen mind and an ability to relate to others without attachment would be valuable. He graduated *magna cum laude* in Reno and matriculated at Georgetown Law School the following fall.

Susan Keiffer grew up in Dubuque, Iowa, the youngest of four girls. Her father, William, was a local physician and her mother, Joan, had been his office nurse until they were married. Both had attended Loras College. The two oldest girls entered the convent and became Sisters of Providence. The sister next to Susan was in the Navy. When Susan graduated from Loras she chose Georgetown to study law.

It was at Georgetown Jim met Susan, another first year student. He had on rare occasions in college taken a girl to a movie or to a party but rarely the same girl. He wasn't shy; girls just didn't interest him. Susan was in two of his classes. She was different, at least from his perspective. She was attractive but it was more than that. She had an *attitude,* a kind of reserve, something *special*. One day in class when he looked at her, their eyes met. She smiled! He waited for her after class. Other classes were starting in five minutes, but they both felt a need to talk more, so they agreed to meet at the end of the day.

They had dinner together and spent hours talking about their past, their families, their plans and expectations for their respective futures. They talked of politics, religion, traveling they did and hoped to do. Jim suddenly realized with dismay he had never opened up like this to anyone in his entire life. "What is happening to me? Is this real? Should I be embarrassed? Have I been rude? What will I feel when I see Susan in class tomorrow?" His thoughts kept coming. He realized he wanted to reach across the table and touch Susan's hand. At that moment Susan reached across the table to Jim's hand and said, "I've never talked as openly and as long to anyone in my life. It's been a delightful evening, Jim. And I should be getting back to the dorm. I have studying to do and so do you."

The remaining weeks and years at Georgetown were suddenly almost over. Susan and Jim were married two months before their graduation with the plan to live happily ever after. Their four parents were in attendance.

Susan and Jim passed the California Bar Examination early in their senior year of law school. After graduation they spent six weeks traveling throughout the United States. They spent a week in San Francisco and while there, they interviewed for associate positions in four different law firms with which they had made previous contact. Jim was accepted as a junior associate in the prestigious firm of Kimberly and Marcus. Susan obtained a similar position in the smaller firm of Kirby and Brown. Before they left San Francisco they rented an apartment not far from the Embarcadero where their respective law offices were located. Within the next thirty days they moved into the apartment and took up their new positions with all the enthusiasm and energy of the pioneers in the gold rush of the 19th Century.

The weeks passed quickly. They reserved Saturdays for odd jobs left from their busy week and on Sundays they tried to spend time together visiting museums, parks, and other recreational activities. The work-week bordered on hectic and weekends evaporated in the pleasurable balm of San Francisco life. They developed satisfying relationships with friends at work and in the apartment complex. The relationships were nourished more by Susan but Jim gradually came to appreciate them. By the time they completed their fourth year in San Francisco they felt secure enough to buy and move into a condominium in a restored area of the Embarcadero.

Prior to marriage they had discussed their attitudes about having a family and agreed they would like to have two or three children. Each of them had siblings and grew up in homes where children were valued. They were sexually active and took no precautions to avoid pregnancy. During the last couple of years, they altered their sexual activities as Susan's doctor recommended to enhance the possibility of a pregnancy. Increasingly disappointed, they tried remedial approaches to intercourse recommended by two different gynecologists with whom they consulted. Sexual compatibility was never a problem. But their sexual life was becoming overshadowed and stressed by their desire to have a child.

They were happy in their marriage, sharing not only a common profession but having similar attitudes politically and socially and spiritually. They were both Christians with church-going backgrounds. Susan's family was Roman Catholic and James's family belonged to the Episcopal Church. They were married by an Episcopal priest in the Georgetown University chapel. As a result of the increasing pressures of law school and impending graduation they stopped attending church services regularly. Since their move to California they failed to continue even irregular attendance.

One Sunday afternoon they were out for lunch and later walking in the park. Susan brought up the subject. "Jim, maybe we should become more active in our religious practice. I think we've been neglecting the spiritual side of life. We don't attend Mass, we don't pray, we never even refer to the subject. Maybe we're getting too caught up in the business side of life."

Jim replied, "You're probably right, Susan, and your comment is not surprising. I've recently had similar thoughts. From time to time I find myself thinking, 'Please, God, won't you send us a child.' Then I wonder if God still knows who I am. Yes, we have been neglectful and what you've said is not only reasonable but a good suggestion. I won't expect praying and attending church is going to bring us a child, but that part of our life is currently missing and somewhere inside I've been increasingly aware of its absence."

The conversation continued and eventually they decided to return to regular Sunday worship and to begin saying night prayers together. When they got home Susan looked up the churches in the area. The closest was an Episcopal Church three blocks from their condo. They decided to attend the service there the following Sunday and if it fulfilled their expectations they would join the parish.

A week or two later after Sunday Service Susan brought up the subject which had become quietly persistent in their lives. "I'm approaching my mid-thirties, Jim, and I realize there are very few alternatives left in our quest for a pregnancy other than a sperm donor or surrogacy. I don't want another man's sperm to produce my child nor do I want some other woman to be artificially inseminated with your sperm. It wouldn't be *our* child. Do you think we should keep trying or should we check to see if there are newer medical procedures?"

Jim replied, "We've been trying. Let's check with your gynecologist once more. It's about our last hope unless the Lord decides on a miraculous intervention now that we're going to church again."

They continued to discuss the matter for much of the afternoon. During the evening they returned to it and in the end agreed to check with Susan's current gynecologist. Susan called the following morning and set up an appointment on Thursday afternoon for both of them. Jim wanted to be with her.

At the Thursday meeting the gynecologist again explained possible procedures. She also went over Susan's health history in detail. She summarized, "Considering Susan's age and, more importantly, the increasing irregularity and discomfort Susan is experiencing during her menses, I do not think Susan is a good candidate for any further medical procedures. I'm so sorry. But I should tell you I've had a number of patients who have given up all hope of a pregnancy. Then to everyone's surprise the woman becomes pregnant and has a perfectly healthy child. The most important lesson I've learned in gynecology is that science falls short of explaining the mysteries of my profession. My practice has strengthened my faith in the deity."

Susan and Jim were disappointed by the doctor's conclusions but as they continued to talk, they agreed they would be patient, continue their prayerful petitions and accept the work of divine providence. They often spoke about how they met and how providential their relationship has always been.

Seven months later a fertility test indicated there was a fetus living in Susan's uterus. On September 16, 1953 Susan gave birth to a six pound ten-ounce healthy baby girl! Susan and Jim were ecstatic with this child of their love, their prayers and the medical guidance they had received. They saw her as their "miracle baby!" During her pregnancy Susan spoke to one of the senior partners at her law firm and requested eighteen months of leave at half pay beginning in her seventh month of pregnancy. (The firm normally authorized maternity leave of nine months at full pay.) So the way was clear for her to spend the next fifteen months with Patricia Ann, the name she and Jim had chosen for their daughter.

The fifteen months passed quickly and Susan was reluctant to return full time to the office. The firm had fewer clients and the senior partner accepted her proposal to return half-time. This allowed Susan to continue devoting quality time to Patricia. A carefully chosen nanny was present the other half days. The atmosphere of the home was *baby-land* for the first four years of Patricia's life.

Susan and Jim were enthralled with parenthood and spent hours talking about their hopes and dreams for their child. When Patty (as they began calling her) was six months old, they drove to Elko, Nevada to introduce to and rejoice with Jim's family over this treasured child. Three months later they drove to Decorah, Iowa to *show off* their special, long-awaited daughter to Susan's family. They had always kept in touch with both their families and both sets of grandparents pleaded for frequent visits. The result: a plan to take a regular two-week summer vacation to include three or four days in Nevada and three or four in Iowa.

Patty was a delightful child with a measure of mischief she easily displayed. She seemed to relish laughter, her own and that of others. She was playful and bright-spirited with family members but was timid around new faces. It took some time for her to accommodate to aunts, uncles and cousins whom she rarely saw. She liked to cuddle with Susan and Jim and especially her maternal grandmother, Joan. By the age of four she had gone through each year meeting all the expectations of statistical charts for child development. All four grandparents saw her as a gifted child, a view carrying the inherent bias of grandparents.

Shortly after Patty's fourth birthday Susan Watson was diagnosed with ovarian cancer. Her discomfort of several months with abdominal bloating and cramps and back pain was sparingly soothed with some over-the-counter remedies she tried, without saying anything to her husband about her discomfort. After all, she was now in her forties so she easily attributed the discomfort to early onset of menopause. As the pain continued to intensify she finally mentioned it to her internist, whose examination suggested her symptoms raised a question of possible ovarian cancer. Three days later Susan had an appointment with her gynecologist who tentatively confirmed the diagnosis, ordered some lab tests and an MRI.

It was time to tell Jim. His initial response was harsh. "Why didn't you tell me when you were having such discomfort? How could you keep this from me? I thought we were honest and open with each other? You should have told me, Susan."

She replied, "I'm so sorry. I really thought my symptoms were due to the onset of menopause. I didn't want to add another burden to your work at the office and I couldn't believe something serious would disrupt our happy life. I thought we paid the price for our happiness when we went through all the hurdles to have Patty. Now I'm worrying about Patty and about you and what effect this will have on our life. Forgive me, Jim, for not telling you sooner."

"Of course, you're forgiven. But please, let's keep communication clear and complete between us. At the moment I'm concerned about you but I'm also thinking about Patty. How much and how are we going to tell her? I suggest we not say anything about it until we know more. We won't have any answers until we see your gynecologist next week and know what the test results show. If it's okay with you I'll go with you for that appointment. I hope and pray it's not as serious as your doctor suggested."

Susan said, "The appointment is next Wednesday afternoon at two. I'd appreciate your coming with me. If it's bad news, I'll need you there."

Concerns about Susan's health weighed heavily on the couple during the waiting time especially on the weekend. They were both more attentive to Patty as if to shield her from the possibility of bad news. Jim took her to a near-by park to play on the slides and swings. They held hands as they walked and Jim kept busy coming up with answers to her multiple questions about *everything*. After lunch Susan played Patty's favorite games with her while Jim did the dishes. That night after Patty was in bed they spent the evening talking about the joy she was in their life and how blessed they were by her presence. They avoided their major concern about Susan's health and how they would tell Patty if Susan has cancer.

The following Wednesday at their meeting, the gynecologist spoke bluntly, "There is no kind way to tell you this. You have ovarian cancer which appears to have spread to lymph nodes in the abdominal area. The next step will be the staging process. I have a friend who is a gynecologic oncologist whom I would encourage you to choose for the staging surgery. During this surgery the abdomen will be opened and biopsies taken of various organs and lymph nodes. After completion of the staging process, we will know if the cancer has spread and to what extent. Staging will give us the information we need to determine appropriate treatment. Do you have any questions? Is what I have said to you clear and understandable?"

Susan responded, "Do you have an informative leaflet of some kind I can take home and look over? I understand generally what you've said but it's difficult to keep most things in my mind these days."

Dr. Byrne handed her a booklet and said, "This will give you more information than you need but it has the material about "staging" which I just mentioned. It has information about treatment but we'll get to that part after the surgery. If you're agreeable to seeing the gynecologic oncologist I mentioned, I'll have my secretary call her office and set up an appointment for you."

Jim and Susan talked it over briefly and agreed. While they continued talking, Dr. Byrne's secretary called for an appointment with Dr. Davis to schedule the cancer staging. Before they left the office, the surgery was scheduled for the following Tuesday morning at eight at the University of California Medical Center. They were advised that Susan might be in the hospital two or three days including the day of surgery.

As they drove home, the diagnosis of cancer was paramount in their minds, followed closely by their concern about Patty and the reality that Susan's illness now needed to be revealed to her. And for the few days Susan is in the hospital who will take care of Patty? Susan suggested she call her mother and ask her to fly from Iowa on the weekend to be with Patty during the hospital time. Jim agreed whole heartedly "if your mother is available." They decided to postpone telling Patty until Susan made the call to see if her mother could come. Her coming would provide a bit of a cushion when they spoke with Patty.

After they were home a while, Jim occupied Patty with her favorite board game while Susan went upstairs and called her mother. When her mother answered, Susan said, "Hi, Mom. I have some news to tell you and I also have a favor to ask. I saw another doctor today and she told me I have ovarian cancer. They want to proceed with some initial minor surgery next Tuesday to find out how serious it is and if it has spread to other sites. I could be in the hospital two or three days. I wonder if you would consider flying here this weekend so Patty can be with you next week while I'm in the hospital. It would be reassuring for her to be with one of her favorite relatives, perhaps her most favorite."

Susan's mother, Joan Kieffer, replied, "Susan dear, I'm so sad to hear this terrible news. I always worry about my children and something always comes up to increase my worries. The word 'cancer' frightens me. You'll all be in my prayers. Of course, I'll be happy to come out. I'll call and get a reservation as soon as I'm off the phone. I presume Saturday or Sunday will work for you."

"Either day would be fine, Mom. Patty will be glad to hear you'll be with her. I'll give you the details of my story when you're here and we can talk quietly to each other. Thanks a bunch, Mom. I love you." Joan called back within the hour and said she would arrive at two fifteen on Saturday afternoon at the Oakland International Airport.

Now it was time for Susan and Jim to talk to four-year-old Patty about what was going to happen next week. They explained to Patty that there were some problems in mommy's "tummy" and a doctor was going to open up her "tummy" next Tuesday to see what might be wrong. Susan said, "Mommy will be in the hospital two or three days. And Grandma Joan is coming here on Saturday and will be with you when I'm in the hospital." The last words got Patty's attention and brought a smile. Grandma Joan was the remedy for parental concerns at least for the present. Grandma Joan arrived on Saturday as scheduled and the rest of that day and the next two days went by awkwardly for the three adults as they tried to hide their sadness and worry from Patty.

On Monday Jim called one of the Senior Partners of the firm and told him what was going on. Jim had no pending court cases so it was agreed he would be in and out of the office during the coming week so he could be with Susan as needed. Tuesday morning, he took Susan to the hospital for the eight a.m. surgery. He planned to spend the day there.

Doctor Davis introduced herself to Jim before Susan was taken to the operating room. It was after eleven when Doctor Davis returned to see him. Doctor Davis asked him to sit with her in a small adjoining room. She began, "The surgery was more extensive than I expected it to be. There is evidence of cancer cells in the ovaries, the peritoneum, and the kidneys.

And several lymph nodes showed metastases. We opened the chest cavity and there was evidence of probable metastatic cells in the left lung. I took biopsies in all these locations. Now we have to wait two or three days before we get the results. Based on what we found I suspect several of the sites will be positive for cancer cells. I think it best to keep Susan here until we have the biopsy reports."

Jim was emotionally devastated by the report. His world suddenly became bleak and tenuous. Doctor Davis said Susan would be awake in a short while so he could visit her. She added, "I will call you directly when we have the biopsy reports and I will arrange to discuss them with you both before Susan goes home."

Jim went to Susan's room and sat with her as she recovered from the anesthesia. When she was awake and alert he told her she would be in the hospital two or three days to recover from the surgery and to wait for results of the biopsy reports. He said that Doctor Davis would meet with both of them before her discharge. Jim dreaded going home knowing he would have to look peaceful and calm in front of Susan's mother and especially for Patty.

The afternoon of the third hospital day Jim was summoned to meet Doctor Davis in Susan's room. The results of the biopsies were grim. Susan had Stage IV peritoneal cancer. Considering the many sites with cancer cells, surgery could not be considered. A course of chemotherapy was recommended with the expectation it would slow the cancer growth. Doctor Davis added, "Cure is not a strong expectation but it is a possibility." She went on to recommend courses of chemotherapy every three weeks for six doses with a rest period in between courses. Each chemotherapy session would take five or six hours. Doctor Davis said she would discharge Susan that afternoon. Susan and Jim were unable to find words for all the questions in their minds as Jim sat by the bed holding Susan's hand.

As they left the hospital and drove home, Susan and Jim realized they were possibly on the road to Susan's death and there was little reason to hope the journey would be long or easy. They held back the emotions that filled their hearts and they took up the concerns which were easier to talk about. How would they give Patty the care she needed and what would they tell her? Who would be with Patty during the lengthy chemotherapy sessions? Who would care for Patty if Susan became increasingly limited in what she was able to do?

They agreed Jim should call Susan's law office the next day and let them know the situation and the need for Susan to resign. When they arrived home they sat in the car for some time to talk about who would take care of Patty. They considered asking Susan's mother and wondered whether or not she would be willing and able to stay. As they discussed it, Susan said, "I'm not sure that would be good for me, Jim, even though it might seem good for Patty. Frankly I'm concerned it might interfere with my relationship with Patty. I should be honest and say I might become jealous of her relationship with my Mom. And if I become increasingly ill and lose some of my mothering abilities, I'm not sure I want my Mom there to fill the gap. I know that sounds selfish and I guess it is."

"It's okay, Susan," Jim replied. "I understand your feelings and I'm not for a minute critical of them. What you say makes sense. In addition, your mother might tend to 'take over' not only with Patty but with the running of the household which could possibly add to my problems as well as yours. And you might be tempted to become dependent on her instead of trying to remain as active and as involved as you can be. People sometimes drift into being more *invalid* than they really are. Your mother's presence might enhance that possibility. How about the nanny we hired when you returned to work halftime after Patty was born? Do you think she would be suitable and available?"

Susan looked relieved as she replied, "I'm glad you can understand and accept how I feel about Mom not being the one. Kit, the nanny, is working out great. She is good with Patty and Patty likes her. She has been flexible and has fit nicely into my schedule of appointments. I didn't ask her to do any housework but she often cleans up the kitchen or tidies some areas when I'm out. I think we should ask her to be here regularly to help out with Patty and help with the house work." Jim agreed. Later that day Susan gave Kit a call and asked about her availability. Kit was happy to accept Susan's request and pleased with the salary offer.

After they were home a while, Susan took her Mom aside and quietly gave her a report about the hospital without getting into details about the gravity of her illness. She talked about it rather lightly and about getting chemotherapy for the next several months with the goal of eliminating the cancer. Joan offered to stay longer and help with Patty but Susan explained they were going to extend Kit's hours and "all will be fine." After tearful goodbyes Saturday morning, Jim took Grandmother Joan to the airport to return to Iowa. Later in the day Susan sat with Patty and told her she would be having some lengthy doctor appointments over the next few months and she was planning to ask Kit to come every day "to be with you when Mom goes to her appointments and to help me with the housework."

Patty was pleased she would have more time with kit, "I like Kit. She's fun to be with. She makes me laugh and plays games with me. She was teaching me some Spanish words because that's the language she speaks with her family."

Susan began her chemotherapy the following month. All seemed to go well for the first year. She maintained her usual activities at home and spent a good bit of time with Patty. She was supportive of Kit and helped her become increasingly familiar with the household duties.

During the second year of chemotherapy, Patty was enrolled in first grade at the Madames of the Sacred Heart School in the Pacific Heights area. She was an eager student responsive to the opportunities to learn. She was comfortable with peers and developed friendships easily. School became somewhat of a haven from the melancholy silently invading her home. Patty was affected by the home environment but was too young to be able to name her feelings or even to express them.

When she began school, her mother would sit with her when she came home and ask all about her day. After several months Susan's chemotherapy became more debilitating and interfered with the mother-daughter ritual. It gradually became Kit with whom Patty discussed her school day. Susan was often in her room lying down when Patty came home. Her mother sometimes came down later and helped prepare dinner. But that too became less frequent and Kit would then prepare the evening meal which Susan might or might not come down to eat. After another year Susan rarely came to dinner. After dinner Patty was always expected to go up to her mother's bedroom and spend a brief and increasingly uncomfortable time with her. Susan showed little interest in Patty's day or school stories. The time actually became difficult for both of them. But the ritual continued.

Jim was there for dinner unless demands at the office kept him overtime which usually occurred three or four nights a week. Whatever time he came home, he would immediately go upstairs to see Susan unless she was in the dining room. After his visit with Susan he would find Patty, give her a kiss and inattentively ask how her day was.

Treatment went on for the next two years with no evidence of improvement. Susan found each treatment increasingly exhausting and incapacitating. She described her situation to Jim as "unbearable" and she wanted to stop the treatments. After discussing it at length Susan reluctantly agreed to continue "for a while." They found a grief counselor in their parish and had several talks with her. It was evident chemotherapy was not improving Susan's condition and there was no clear reason to believe it was prolonging her life. The grief counselor helped them openly discuss their thoughts and feelings about Susan's desire to stop treatment, and she enabled Jim to understand and to accept Susan's choice. They discontinued treatment.

Susan's attitude changed gradually but markedly over the next three months. She began to say the diagnosis was "inaccurate" and it was "a serious mistake" to have participated in chemotherapy. She even tried to convince Jim she never had cancer. She made light of it when she talked to Patty and told her "someday your father and all the doctors will have to admit they were wrong." Her persistent denial made it difficult for family and friends to talk with her when the subject was introduced. And Susan typically introduced it. As a result, those who watched her slow deterioration found it increasingly challenging to visit or to offer support. Among themselves they talked about her denial as a deeply entrenched emotional problem. On rare occasions Susan told Jim that God "protected" her from the illness the doctors said she had. Jim discussed the extent of her distorted thinking with close family members and a few friends.

At the same time her physical condition was rapidly deteriorating. It was an effort for her to take care of her personal hygiene. She often stayed in her nightgown all day, sometimes wearing a robe. She rarely sat at the table during meal time. She went in the kitchen off and on through the day and picked out a little food she felt was *safe to eat*, as she described it. She kept losing weight.

At one point Jim called Dr. Davis to ask about the changes in Susan's behavior. After hearing his comments, Dr. Davis said it was likely the cancer had metastasized to Susan's brain and was the cause of her delusional thinking and behavioral deterioration.

Susan Watson died at home after being on Hospice Care for seven months. The family home had taken on a mortuary atmosphere the past three years. It was a bewildering and lonely time for Patty who was a month from her eighth birthday when Susan died. Susan's funeral was a numbing experience for Patty. The four grandparents came and several aunts and uncles. The maternal grandmother focused on Patty and was her only comforting companion during that time. Jim concentrated on details of the vigil evening, the funeral Mass, the burial rite at the grave site and the reception that followed. His resulting inattention to Patty was an off-shoot of this involvement. It was understandable to everyone *except Patty.*

Kit had continued to serve the family needs during the past four years, focusing her attention on Patty and increasingly assuming full duty as cook and housekeeper, roles that gradually enlarged for her as Susan became increasingly incapacitated and eventually bed-ridden.

Jim agonized over Susan's death even though he was aware of its imminence for months. Accompanying his sorrow was his determination to be attentive to Patty's heightened need over the loss of her mother. But his attempts to console her were awkward. Jim couldn't keep from tears when he said anything to Patty about her mother. His tears confused Patty as he reached out to comfort her. Jim was unaware that Patty had emotionally separated from her mother long before her mother's death. Susan's physical withdrawal and loss of sensitivity for her daughter's needs had created a chasm which death now occupied. Jim's grief interfered with his ability to sense Patty's lack of grief. Thus began a growing distance between them.

Kit was another factor in the equation. She had always been affectionate toward Patty and became increasingly so during Susan's deterioration. Kit showed an interest in Patty's homework, but more importantly asked her about her friends at school. Patty became comfortable talking to Kit about the girls she liked and those she disliked. She talked about her teachers and especially Sister Dorothy whom she described as a friend. There was little contact with boys since her school was a private school for girls. On occasion her school had a spelling bee or a history competition or a speaking contest with a nearby private school for boys, St. Thomas Academy. Patty enjoyed talking with Kit about those days and how exciting it was to see the boys and she would talk about the boys she thought were "cute."

The distance between Patty and her father became more noticeable to Jim and he tried to bridge the gap. He would ask her what she was studying and what grades she was getting. When she brought her report card home each month, he would go over it carefully with her and focus on the poorer grades, raising questions about the reasons for them. He sometimes asked if he could go over her homework with her but she declined his offers. He asked general questions about her teachers and about her classmates. In return he got general answers, "They're fine" or "They're all right." She offered no details and he asked for none. She didn't explain that the poor grade in science was from a teacher whom everyone disliked, or the good grade in math was partly due to her friend, Joyce, with whom she studied during lunch time. These were things she spontaneously talked about to Kit. No need to talk to her father because he would only criticize her for her "attitude."

The years went on: Jim struggling with his own loneliness, trying to develop a warm and communicating relationship with Patty, and keeping up with an increasingly busy law practice. Within a year of Susan's death Jim asked Kit if she was available to move into their condo and offered her the spare bedroom with a private bath. Kit was delighted. She was currently living with her mother and three siblings in a small apartment. Jim agreed she could spend nights with her family or friends as long as she arranged for them in advance and at times when he was certain to be home.

Patty was about to graduate from grade school. Jim urged her to continue with the Madames of the Sacred Heart High School. Patty was determined to go to St. Thomas Academy, a coeducational High School. Jim tried to discuss the decision with her. He said, "When you were still very young, your Mom and I used to sit and talk about your future, where you would go to school and what kind of profession or work you would someday do. We had our dreams. One of them was that you would be educated by the Madames of the Sacred Heart through high school. Your Mom went to school with them in Iowa and always said it gave her a wonderful educational foundation. I wish you would accept that plan for the sake of me and your Mom."

Patty replied rather strongly, "Dad, I'm not here to fulfill a dream you and Mom had when I was a baby. I'm tired of the stilted piety and teaching of the Madames. I'd like to be in a school where there are boys. And most of my friends are going to St. Thomas."

Jim replied, "Would you at least think about it some more before you decide? You're only thirteen now and it seems to me it's kind of young to be making a decision which will certainly impact your future. Mom and I always wanted what was best for you. I don't want to have to insist."

"Dad, I don't want to have to resist. I've been getting good, no very good, grades. They will not continue if I go to the Madames. Those you cannot control. I think you better give it some more thought."

Jim was irritated with Patty's pert response and attitude. "Tuition in private schools is expensive. I think you should be grateful for the educational opportunity you have and that I'm paying for. The note of rebellion in your comments irritates me. It's not respectful."

"Dad, I'm not trying to irritate you, but whether you like it or not I need to make some choices for myself. This is one of them. And there will be more. I'm sorry if it makes you unhappy." This was the first open sign of the growing conflict between Patty and her father.

During the years at St. Thomas, Patty continued to have good grades and her social life expanded to include naturally formed groups of boys and girls. Late in her junior year she began dating one boy regularly. Jim insisted she have Frank come to the house to meet him before she could go on an individual date with him. Frank and Patty arranged a date so he came to pick Patty up and dutifully to meet her father. It was a formality Jim insisted on and even though it gave him no real information about Frank it eased his mind. Patty and Frank continued to date throughout her senior year. He often spent time at the house with Patty, so Jim saw him rather frequently. Jim was not pleased with Frank's shoulder length hair, his overly cordial attitude toward Jim and his possessive attitude toward Patty.

After she dated Frank a few months, Jim decided he should have a "fatherly talk" with Patty. It proved to be an awkward time for him and an irritating time for Patty. Jim spoke about the dangers of using alcohol and/or drugs and expanded on his reasons for mentioning them. He spoke about the impropriety and the sin of sexual intimacies, the dangers of disease and the life-changing results of pregnancy. Patty had heard it all before in less direct form from the Madames and in more direct form from the Jesuits at St. Thomas. Jim never thought to talk about peer pressure, the most significant piece of the decision-making process for Patty, Frank and their peers.

Patty graduated with a 3.8 average and was class Valedictorian. Jim bought her a new Chevrolet for graduation. She had her driver's license and had been using Jim's car on occasion. Jim told her he was proud of her success and offered to pay for a trip to see his parents in Nevada and then to visit her maternal grandparents in Iowa. Patty said she found a job in a jewelry store preparing jewelry for the counter displays. Jim was not only surprised but irritated because she had not discussed the summer job with him. She would be eighteen in August but she was still living at home and he felt he had a right to be told in advance about her summer plans. He told her his thoughts. She replied, "I'll have a week vacation in the summer and if you are willing to make the trip to my grandparents I'll go with you if it's the week of my vacation". Jim said he had not decided about the summer. Before she left the room Patty walked over to Jim, hugged him, kissed him and said, "Thank you for the car Dad. It is a wonderful gift. I was totally surprised, and I am also totally grateful." Jim didn't know then that someday he would often sadly remember that moment.

Coincidentally with Patty's graduation Jim was promoted to senior associate at Kimberly and Marcus. The satisfaction of his promotion was dimmed by his realization he had no one significant with whom to celebrate. Susan was gone and his relationship with Patty had grown increasingly distant. He didn't even mention the promotion to Patty.

Now father and daughter faced a new challenge. What college and what major? Jim came from a conservative and rather traditional family. Although he didn't directly seek guidance from his parents he usually talked to them about his plans as he moved through high school and college. He had no appreciation of the current turmoil in most young persons (ages sixteen to twenty-four) and the sense of unrest they felt in the world they faced. The country was still recovering from World War II and the futile waste of lives in the Korean conflict. It was the time of draft dodging, student riots, homosexual "outing,", and psychedelics. "Hippie-rebellion" was under way.

In January of her senior year Patty applied to four colleges on the Pacific coast. She mentioned it to her father who simply replied, "I'm glad you're taking care of it." He remembered his chagrin over the choice of high schools and was determined not to get into an argument about college attendance. Patty received an acceptance at all four colleges and chose City College of San Francisco. It had a good liberal arts program and several of her friends, including Joyce, were going there. Patty felt there was plenty of time to decide about her future. Frank decided to attend the San Francisco State University to study psychology.

Patty began her summer job a week after graduation. She worked at McGregor Jewelry, a well-known shop in the Embarcadero. She worked in a separate room assembling jewelry pieces from fixed designs in preparation for display. She adapted quickly to the job and after three weeks she began to modify some designs or create one purely her own. She showed Scott, the store manager, the initial modifications and her personal designs. He was pleased with her work and encouraged her to continue making the unique pieces when she had free time.

Patty's vacation week was scheduled for mid-July. Since the earlier discussion with her father about a trip to see the grandparents, he said nothing further regarding summer plans. Frank was living at home with his parents and on occasion helping his father in his roofing business.

When Patty mentioned her week vacation to Frank, he suggested they drive to Vancouver, British Columbia and visit Vancouver Island.

Patty didn't tell her father the next week would be her vacation week. Actually they rarely saw each other. Jim left for work before Patty was up and ready for breakfast. Patty saw Frank two or three nights a week and often came home after her father was in bed. Patty usually ate breakfast with Kit and the two of them often ate dinner together because Jim frequently came home late from the office. The three of them normally ate together on Saturdays and Sundays and their conversations rarely covered anything personal. Patty found her meals alone with Kit were by far more comfortable.

The Saturday morning Patty left for vacation, her father was still in bed. She simply left him a note. "Dad, Going on vacation with Frank. Taking my car. See you when I get back next weekend."

Patty and Frank had a good trip and enjoyed the time together. They shared the driving and most of the expenses. They jabbered on about all kinds of things that came to mind. They spoke seriously about marriage as a possibility, but they agreed if it happened, it would not be until both finished college. Patty acknowledged it was the first time she felt she was in love and told Frank he was her first sexual partner. Frank chose not to reveal any information about his past nor did she press him to do so. They talked about whether or not they would want children and found that neither saw children as a necessary part of married life. During the week Patty noted several occasions when Frank seemed more irritable and impatient with himself and with her. At the time she saw no reason for it and hoped this wasn't a fault she just hadn't noticed before.

They found mutual interests as they walked around in Vancouver and then as they explored the Gardens and trails and shops of Vancouver Island. On the drive home they agreed it was a satisfying trip and helped them know each other better. They spent much of the travel time talking about where they would like to go the next time they could schedule a week together.

After she dropped Frank off, Patty drove up to her door about four o'clock Sunday afternoon. When she came in, she called, "Hello, everybody. I'm home." Her father was watching baseball and just waved his hand. Kit came out of the kitchen and gave her a hug. Kit said, "I'm planning dinner for five o'clock. It'll be nice to have you at the table." Patty noted a possible inference in Kit's words. She wondered how the meals went with just Jim and Kit present.

When they sat down for dinner, no one spoke for several minutes. It was Kit who was the ice-breaker with, "Did you enjoy your trip?" Patty responded, saying where they went and how enjoyable it was.

Jim looked up from his plate and said, "Did you two sleep together?"

Patty put her fork down and looked at him. "That's none of your business, Dad. But 'yes' I did and 'yes' we had sex and 'yes' he used a condom and "yes" we will continue to have sex. You are rude and out of line to ask the question in the first place and in the second place to ask it with Kit here. Would you like to broadcast to the world that your only daughter is a fallen woman? I presume that's how you see me now."

Jim said nothing, finished his dinner in silence, left the table and went to his room. When he was gone, Kit said, "I'm sorry Patty. Your dad just can't help being over-protective. I'm a woman. It was no news to me. Be careful, Honey, don't get pregnant."

Later when Patty was in her room putting her traveling clothes away, there was a knock on her door. When she opened it, her father was waiting and said, "I'm sorry, Patty. You're right; it isn't any of my business. Maybe I did it because you left on your trip without saying goodbye." He turned away quickly and went to his room.

Before the fall term started at City College, Scott approached Patty one day at work and said, "Patty, would you consider working here on Saturdays when the semester begins? You're good at what you do, better than anyone we've had in that job. And if you're willing maybe you'll give us some additional hours when the holidays come." Scott offered her a good hourly rate. She was pleased with the offer and accepted it. It would be good to have some extra money she could save for future needs. When she started college her father agreed to pay for tuition, books and any other college fees for four years. In addition, he gave her one hundred dollars a month for personal needs. Patty saw it as a generous decision on her father's part and frequently expressed her gratitude (when they were on good speaking terms.)

Once classes started the weeks passed quickly; Patty was surprised each time Saturday came and she was back at her desk in the jewelry store. She enjoyed the challenges of college classes and found herself spending one to three hours each night studying. She was taking her first Spanish class and enjoyed framing conversations with Kit in Spanish when she talked about events at the college. Kit, in turn, was increasingly interested in hearing about the college classes. One evening she asked Patty if the college had evening courses and did Patty think Kit might be able to attend. Kit said she completed high school in a Spanish-speaking neighborhood where she lived, but much of it was difficult and she continued to struggle with understanding and writing English. She had arrived from Ecuador only a year before she began high school.

The next day Patty brought home college brochures about evening classes with additional information about the history and record of the college, a profile of the racial mix at the college, the country of origin of their students, and data related to financial help for underprivileged students and students from outside the United States. Kit responded like the typical child in a candy shop. She caressed the glossy covers and looked through each booklet page by page, following the large print with her finger and studying each picture. Patty sat with Kit for over an hour explaining and clarifying each item that might be of interest and of help to promote and satisfy Kit's educational dreams. By the end of the evening Kit gave Patty a long embrace and expressed her gratitude so profusely she found herself saying it in Spanish and then in translation. Kit was anxious to talk to her family about it, so when Jim came home later she arranged to be away two evenings of the following week.

The college year ended and Patty returned to her regular schedule at McGregor's. Frank was spending the summer as he did a year ago. He lived at home and occasionally helped his father. Patty asked why he didn't get a full time job. He said this gave him more freedom and more flexibility in his life and his father really didn't need him on a regular basis. Patty asked, "What do you do with your free time? Why is it so precious to you?"

Frank answered, "I hang out with friends. We talk, tell our lies, imagine our futures and smoke a little pot. Occasionally we might see a movie or watch some T.V. in a 'free house.' Oh, a 'free house' is a house where no family members are home. Sometimes it's a place to party. We've started going to the Haight-Ashbury district and just walk around looking at all the weirdos. I'll take you there some Saturday. It's an interesting place."

Patty commented, "I didn't know you smoked marijuana, Frank. How come you never mentioned it before? Is it a regular thing you do? Did you smoke pot when we were away last summer?"

Frank was casual about it all. "I've smoked a joint off and on with friends for three or four years. I never mentioned it because it's no big deal. There's no addiction involved. They say it leads to more serious drugs, cocaine, etc. That's a lot of propaganda as far as I'm concerned. And to answer your question, I didn't have any source when we were on vacation and I forgot to bring any with me. That may account for some of my irritability and moodiness in Canada."

Patty was surprised by almost everything Frank just said. Maybe not surprised but disappointed. She noted his absence of ambition and any real focus on the future. She knew a lot of high school students smoked marijuana but wondered why Frank never mentioned it. She couldn't imagine a bunch of young guys hanging out together day after day in the summer and not getting into some kind of trouble. Frank apparently had little or no interest in sports. He never went to games or talked about watching sports on T.V.

After a few minutes of silence Patty said, "You mentioned a 'free house' as a place to party. What kind of *parties* do you have?"

"Oh, just a few guys hanging out, some pot, some beer, some bragging about their exploits," Frank answered.

Patty said, "Am I one of your *exploits,* Frank?"

A quick reply, "Of course not. Why all the questions? You know I love you and you have nothing to worry about. I'll tell you what we should do. Next Saturday why don't we go to Haight-Ashbury so you can see for yourself what a crazy, wild place it is?"

Patty agreed to go, so they made their plans. They arrived in the area a little past noon. Patty was overwhelmed by the wild clothes on some and the lack of clothes on others, the number of individuals playing banjos, drums, violins, guitars and what-all on different street corners. All the music seemed to have the same sort of rhythm and quality and *loudness.* People were laughing and talking, some without listeners, some dancing wildly on the sidewalks, the streets, the alleys. Some were singing with the music and without, songs familiar and strange. Every two or three minutes someone would shout "love" or "peace" or "freedom" or "life" or "fuck it all" or some obscenity. The streets were filled with kiosks and tables with people selling a variety of things, things they made or stole or found in the trash, collections of books or jewelry or medals and even rosary beads and, of course, (from the stash) drugs.

Patty stopped and stared when she first observed the scene. She was enthralled by the joy and happiness and wildness and freedom and rebellion and peace that seemed to drift through the air. It was initially riveting yet somewhat disorienting. Then it felt like it was **too much** of what it was. She gradually separated herself internally and regained a more stable sense of self. She took Frank's hand as they walked around.

Almost everyone smiled or nodded or spoke to everyone else. There were moments when she felt like everyone knew her. There was no anonymity. They were all "one." Occasionally someone would call Frank by name. In one group of about ten guys and girls gathered together they seemed to *actually know* Frank and spoke or made comments. "Where'd you get the chick?" "Whose coop did you raid?" "What "safe house" are you going to use?" Most of them laughed, but Patty noted one tall red haired girl wasn't even smiling.

After they walked away Patty asked Frank what a 'safe house' was. He said, "It's an abandoned house that is available for shelter. There are lots of abandoned houses in the area and a lot of the people you see walking around here don't have homes they go to. They go to abandoned houses to sleep, to hide from the police or family members, to get high, to have sex, or just to find solitude. Occasionally a few people may move in together and fix the place up a little and live there. It's called a 'safe house' because anyone can use it as long as you leave it the way you found it. A guy and his girl can go in, have sex and leave. You are 'safe' there."

Patty and Frank walked on looking at things as they passed. They were watching some birds in a shop window when Frank said, "I'll be right back. I just want to say 'hello' to the guy at the kiosk over there." Patty watched. As Frank approached, the man looked at him and gave a meaningful thumbs-up gesture. They stood and talked for a few minutes. Patty noticed a sort of hand shake or maybe an exchange of something between the two. Or was it just her increased suspicion in this unusual and almost scary environment? People called out "peace" and "love," but there was a sense of danger and uncertainty in Patty's mind.

As they walked away, Patty asked, "A friend of yours?"

Frank didn't reply immediately. After they walked on a bit, he said, "He's not really a friend but we stay in touch. I got a few pills from him just now. I'll give you one and I'll take one just to show you there's no harm in them. Just put it in your mouth and swallow it."

Patty: "I won't take it 'till I know what it is. So what is it?"

Frank: "Phil, the guy I spoke to, calls them Pep pills. They're nothing dangerous. I take them often. It's like taking a big cup of coffee. It perks you up a bit, brightens your day, increases your energy. It won't hurt you I guarantee. At least try it, no harm."

Although Patty was reluctant she felt she could trust Frank and rely on what he said. She swallowed the pill. They walked along another twenty minutes and when they passed Hamburger House, Frank suggested they get a hamburger and a coke. Patty was hungry and agreed. There was a big sign in the window, No Pigs Served. Frank explained the sign referred to policemen.

After they finished eating Frank asked Patty if she was ready to start home. As they left they walked through a small garden-park area toward the car. Patty was aware of feeling a little giddy and she remarked to Frank how bright green the grass was and it was hurting her eyes to look at it. She said, "Maybe I'm going blind." She grabbed Frank's arm and almost shouted, "Everything is getting bright and shiny. Your face shines like an angel's face. I'm frightened. Hold onto me because I'm drifting off into space. I'm scared. I know someone followed us from the village. I saw them hiding in the bushes we just passed. They plan to kill me." The panic words came quickly, one on top of the other. Some were loud, almost shouts; then they were whispered.

Frank put his arms around her and held her tight. He quietly and calmly spoke, "You'll be okay, Patty. It's your first 'trip' on the LSD express. Try to relax and ride along. It has some highs and some lows but it's a wonderful experience."

Patty began again, "Oh, it's so beautiful. I'm drifting over the world. It's smooth and peaceful. The music is strange but lovely. I don't know who's playing. Do you know? I see the band over there and a red-haired girl with wings and a tail is singing. But I'm afraid I'm dying. The music is for my funeral. Is this my funeral Frank? I can feel my heart racing. It will stop and then I'll be dead."

With his arm around her, Frank helped Patty move to a bench in the area. They sat there together while Patty's psyche went traveling on through the heights and depths, the delights and terrors of LSD land. Frank sat with closed eyes and enjoyed a more familiar land of ecstasy.

It was almost an hour before Patty was calmer and able to recognize what was real and what was not. Frank was still in a blissful state but more communicative. Patty felt unsteady and "dreamy" but dangerously decided she was stable enough to drive. She took Frank home. On the way little was said that made sense. She was realistic enough to know trying to discuss anything with Frank now would be a waste of time. She stopped the car at his house and he got out without a word. As she drove home Patty felt betrayed and violated by Frank for giving her the pill she now knew was LSD.

She was grateful her father wasn't in the house when she arrived. She was still not feeling confident about what she was doing or saying. She was aware enough to realize that her feelings, thoughts, and reactions could be off-target. She spoke to Kit for a few minutes when she entered; but shortly said, "I'm tired so I think I'll lie down for a while." It was after five when she woke. She stayed in her room until after seven and then went down and found something to eat in the kitchen. Kit was out for the evening and her father was in the den watching TV. She went back to bed.

Patty got up and went to the nine o'clock Mass Sunday morning. She had not been going to Mass since her mother died. It was more on impulse that she went this day. She felt somewhat disoriented through the morning hours. She spent most of the day wandering through different areas of the Embarcadero and reviewing the events of the prior day. She was still angry at Frank for giving her LSD without telling her what it was. But as she reviewed the experience, she found the memories beguiling and beckoning. She remembered a serenity and pleasure beyond anything she ever felt before. She remembered the brilliance of trees and sky in a world of splendor. She remembered fear and distress, but couldn't remember the danger. And she wondered what it would be like to take it again. The possibility came to mind repeatedly through the following week.

Frank made no contact for several days which was unusual. They usually saw each other every two or three nights. On Friday he called and said he was going to be away for the weekend, going with his father to pick up some equipment in Portland. He was about to leave so the conversation was brief. Patty felt there was a difference in their exchange but she was also aware several of the week's experiences seemed unusual. One event of the week dominated her thinking. On Monday she had time to work on designs of her own. She made two pieces of jewelry which were highly creative and brought comments from the store manager and other personnel. A recurring explanation came to Patty. She was drifting in her mind into the LSD experience as her hands fashioned the work in "a meditative state of mind." It left her wondering. Did she have some special gift brought out by this "mind expanding drug?"

On Friday afternoon Scott came to her work station and asked if she would like to come in on Saturday. Almost without thinking, Patty said,

"No, I have other plans." As soon as he walked away she knew she was going back to Haight-Ashbury alone tomorrow.

On Saturday Patty decided not to drive but to take a bus to the area. She arrived about the same time she and Frank got there a week ago. Nothing was changed. The people, the music, the noise, the kiosks, the shouts, the confusion: it was all there. She again felt the peace and the warmth but also the taint of danger and fear. She had been there about an hour when a female voice called her name above the noisy background. She looked around and there was her college classmate, Joyce, waving her hand. They were in grade school together and remained friends and continued to study together at City College. They embraced and immediately struck up a conversation about why each was there.

Joyce said she had been coming off and on for the past several months and by now felt quite at home in the area. She often hung out with a couple of other young women who were living in a "saved house" a few blocks from where they were standing. Joyce explained that a "saved house" is an abandoned house that any number of people take over and live in. They chatted away as they walked through the busy streets. Before long they were in the area where a week ago Frank stopped at the kiosk and bought the "Pep Pills." Joyce suddenly interrupted their conversation. "Give me a minute. I have to pick up something at that kiosk."

Patty put her hand on Joyce's arm, "Do you use LSD? I ask because my boyfriend bought some there when we were here last Saturday."

Joyce didn't hesitate. "I've been using since my senior year in high school. Lately I pick it up almost every Saturday and spend most of the weekend in the Land of Oz. Did you try it? Do you want me to get you some? The guy calls them 'Pep Pills' or 'Trip Tickets.' That's what you ask for."

Patty said, "Frank gave me one a week ago. The effect was frightening but also exhilarating. I was hearing and seeing scary stuff but there was also a peace and sense of everlasting joy. I was drawn here today by the thought of trying it one more time."

Joyce responded, "There'll always be a 'one more time,' my friend. I'll treat this time and get you one." At the kiosk Joyce told the dealer, "The young woman with me is a friend of mine. She's good, no strings. She's good to buy."

Patty and Joyce each took the innocent looking little tablet. They continued talking as they walked along. Joyce talked about problems with her family. She knows her father is unfaithful to her mother. She expects them to separate when her mother learns of his infidelity and Joyce is about to arrange for her mother to discover the news. Both parents constantly criticize Joyce for her slovenly behavior, her poor grades, and some of the girlfriends she brings to the house. Joyce talked about the possibility of moving out. Patty asked where she would go if she left.

Joyce went on, "I've been thinking of moving to the "saved house" here where my friends are living. They have asked me to come and they have enough room. Betty is lesbian and Janet is straight so they sleep in separate rooms and bring 'pick-ups' in as desired. I'm 'butch' so I'd pair up with the Betty if I joined them. Why don't you join us? They'd welcome someone who is straight to pair up with Janet. It wouldn't be costly. They pay no rent but they keep up on the water, gas and electric bills. It would give you a lot of freedom which is what it's going to give me."

Just then Patty noticed a mixed group of young people laughing and talking on a side street they were passing. Frank was in the group with his back turned toward Patty. His arm was around the waist of the red haired girl Patty saw the day she was there with Frank. She decided to think about it later. There were more important things now.

Patty and Joyce stopped for a beef burger and a soda and then agreed to leave the area. Joyce had her car so she offered to drive Patty home. It was fortunate Joyce had been at Patty's house before because during the drive Patty's LSD trip began. The red traffic lights were shouting curses at them and threatening to kill them. Joyce turned into an angel and read bible verses from the dash board. She thought the car was stopped and the houses were all moving down the street. She laughed and sang one of the songs she just heard. Then came, "How does your car fly above the streets? It feels like an airplane but it makes a frightening noise and we're going to fall and crash." She covered her face with her hands and then was suddenly singing again and laughing.

Joyce was having some of the same feelings but was familiar with the experience and could maintain sufficient contact to drive safely to Patty's house. As Patty tried to compose herself to get out of the car, Joyce said, "Stay cool, Patty. Enjoy the highs and just hang on when the scary comes. Think about moving in with me and my two friends. There is peace and love to be found."

When Patty entered the house her father was sitting in the living room reading the morning paper. Patty called a cheery, "Hi Dad, how are they hanging?" as she went over and kissed the top of his head. He looked up in surprise and immediate irritation.

He put the paper down and stood up. "What are you so cheerful about? I never heard you talk like that before. Where have you been? Have you been drinking? Have you taken drugs? What's going on with you?"

Patty was poorly prepared for the encounter. "Hey, daddyo, been out doing the town. How about you? Did you have any fun this morning playing with the paper? Or playing with yourself? Is that where you get your kicks? Or don't you have any? How about a lady friend? Maybe it would improve your disposition."

It was clear to Jim that Patty was under the influence of alcohol or drugs of some kind. "Clearly you've been abusing something to come in at this time of day and to behave as you're doing. You're disheveled, your pupils are as big as saucers, and your comments are insulting. I'd suggest you go to bed and sleep it off before things get worse. We will talk about this later when you return to your senses; but let me tell you now, 'No one in this house is going to live here and abuse alcohol or drugs of any kind.'"

"Okay, Pops. I'll catch you later when you're a little more stable and when I'm in the mood for a sermon. Happy dreams!"

Patty went to the fridge and picked up some food. She went to her room and did not come out until the next morning. She was in the kitchen eating pancakes and talking to Kit when her father returned from Sunday Mass. He stopped by and said, "I'll be in the living room. I need to talk to you when you've finished eating."

Before Jim came home Patty told Kit about the major events of Saturday. Kit expressed her own fears about substance abuse, especially narcotics or LSD. She admitted she had no personal experience with any drugs, but some of her friends and family members were caught using drugs, were arrested and are still in jail.

Patty finished her breakfast and went to the living room. Her father motioned her to a chair he had placed facing himself. He began, "I assume you remember some of what happened yesterday when you returned home from your drug escapade. I won't ask you for any details because you possibly don't remember much of it and if you do remember you are likely to lie about it. I have, more than once, talked to you about the dangers of drug use. You obviously have chosen to ignore my warnings, but you can have no doubt about my attitude and my position. As long as you are living in this house, I forbid you to use narcotics of any kind and LSD which apparently is equally or possibly more dangerous than narcotics. I won't make the same edict about alcohol unless you use it to excess. Do I make myself clear?"

Patty was silent for a time considering what to say. "I used LSD yesterday, Dad. It was the second time. I admit its use does have an attraction. It makes me feel more productive and more in touch with the world. I don't remember what I said to you yesterday when I came in. I was pretty high. I'm sorry if I was offensive. I'll think seriously about what you just said. I've given some thought to moving out and trying to find my way in life on my own. Everything I do now seems to need to pass your muster."

Jim replied, "My immediate reaction is to ask you to stay. I know we don't spend much time together but I would miss you greatly if you left. I think I can understand your thoughts about being on your own. If you decide to leave I will continue our arrangement and will pay for all college expenses including books. I will continue the additional allowance as long as you remain in school. If you go I would be grateful if you keep in touch and come for dinner occasionally." Jim stood, gave Patty a kiss on the forehead and went for a walk.

Patty was grateful for the peaceful discussion and was surprised her father was able to understand her thoughts about being on her own. But she did feel some rejection in his readily supportive comment about her moving out.

When she was at work Monday morning, Frank called. When she heard his voice, she said, "I'm really quite busy. Call me this evening." End of conversation. Patty wanted more time to think and decide how she wanted to handle her relationship with him. As she reflected on the weekend: seeing Frank, the time with Joyce, the "trip," the talk with her father, it all gave her a different perspective on life. Her world was enlarging and at the same time feeling less secure. The second year of college would start in another two weeks. She had never questioned the trajectory she set her sights on when she finished high school. She planned to finish college. Then what? She had no particular goals in life. She and Frank talked of marriage but today that seemed an immature objective. Maybe she should go off on her own, spread her wings and see what fate brings. By the end of the day her mind was still drifting through an assortment of possibilities.

Frank called her about seven that evening. Patty had not decided what she planned to say or do about Frank. After their "hellos" were said, the conversation was brief.

Patty: "How was your weekend?"

Frank: "It was okay. I hate it when my father wants me to help him on weekends, because I don't get to see you."

Patty: "Did the red head go with you?"

Frank: "What red head?"

Patty: "The red head you were with at Haight-Ashbury on Saturday."

Frank: "I wasn't—So I guess you saw me there. It wasn't anything important. I was just clearing up some loose ends from the past."

Patty: "Bullshit, Frank. Don't ever call me again. Have the same lousy life you've been living. Goodbye."

When Patty ended the call she felt positive about herself and the decision she just made. It was quick. It was final. She was feeling confident.

The rest of the work week kept Patty busy, but amid the busyness her thoughts still focused on possibilities ahead. Her mind kept coming back to the Haight-Ashbury scene. What was the attraction? She couldn't pin it down. She couldn't define it or uncover it. Yes, the LSD experience was part of it. But there was also an atmosphere of friendliness, an infusion of love in the streets.

College classes were starting next mid-week so she would go back to working Saturdays at the jewelry store. This would be the last Saturday she'd be free to go to Haight-Ashbury. She called Joyce to ask about going with her. Joyce said she'd be glad to have her company and suggested they get together with Janet and Betty, the two women who shared a saved house and were open for roommates. Patty was delighted and said she had been wondering about the possibility of meeting the other two.

Patty looked forward to Saturday and without doubt LSD was an expectation for the day. She questioned her own behavior. Was this leading to addiction? Certainly *for some people* it was apparently addictive. There was enough written in the press about it. But Timothy Leary, a psychology professor no less, who espoused its use, said it opened the mind to a new philosophy of life and a new age of enlightenment. She decided her mental processes had benefitted from LSD use. She recalled the more rational discussion with her father when she talked to him about her future a week ago. She was pleased with her decision about Frank and thought she handled it well. And there were the unusual pieces of jewelry she recently shaped. Had some new light dawned in her life?

Patty was happy Joyce picked her up on Saturday. She wasn't sure she wanted to drive assuming she would probably "get high." Joyce talked freely about her relationship with Janet and Betty. Betty "hit" on her shortly after the three became friends and she and Betty were spending "private times" together. She expected they would continue their sexual relationship for some time. Then she added, "Until someone else comes along." She continued, "On the other hand, Janet is more reserved, straight and currently continues to attend a secretarial school in the city. Betty is unemployed but may be involved in 'the trade,' referring to drug distribution."

The four young women got together at Tim's Place, a sort of barn like room with plain tables and chairs and a bar up front where you could buy a variety of fast food lunches (and other items if you knew the right people). Various musicians with or without singers wandered in from time to time and after entertaining for about twenty minutes would pass the hat and leave. During lunch the four of them got to know each other, talking about their backgrounds, their families, and plans for the future. They were unanimous regarding plans. No one professed any other than to "turn on, tune in, and drop out," one might say "to follow the Leary creed." Patty felt hesitant when they talked about the Leary creed but verbally signed on without a show of reluctance. Inwardly she wondered where all this was taking her. This was not the world of her family, of her background, of her faltering religious beliefs or of the goals she had a few weeks ago.

After spending a couple of hours over their food and their stories, Joyce said, "How about we pick up an assortment and go to your house and we'll show Patty the 'digs' and get high?" Unanimous agreement came readily.

Janet said, "Why don't we each chip in ten or twelve dollars and let Betty make the buy? She can get us a good deal and we'll leave the assortment up to her." Within a few seconds Betty was "flush" and on her way to see Phil.

Betty soon returned with a small paper bag in her hand and a crooked smile on her face. They left Tim's Place for the home of Betty and Janet. After the first two or three uncluttered blocks, Patty counted eight more blocks of dirty streets, shoddy houses, an occasional rusty wreck of an abandoned car, and smelly trash. There were no children in the area, but they met a number of sloppy guys and girls about their own age, many looking dazed or drunk. They were not disorderly or discourteous. Some would wave or greet them with "love" or "peace" or "happy day, sister." Patty was thinking, "It's not a scary place but it is sure a stinky one."

The house was a small one story building on a lot about twice the size of the house itself. When they entered, Janet said, "This is our mansion.

We moved in about four months ago. The house was vacant and apparently had been vacant for a year or more. There were piles of trash and garbage in the house but no other sign of previous residents. But there were plenty of resident mice and rats. Betty and I took turns walking around the area and casing out the house and the neighborhood for about three months before we decided to move in. Then we just came with blankets, some extra clothes and a few things we could eat from cans. We brought poison for the rats and mice. Oh, we also brought a broom and cleaned up what we could without water.

"After we hung out in the house for almost a month, we went to the gas, electric and water companies to get services turned on. No questions asked other than proof of citizenship. There was an initial turn-on fee and then the monthly bills which total about thirty-five dollars. We keep usage to a minimum. We've expanded our furniture as you can see by the sofa, coffee table and two arm chairs. The kitchen is small but adequate. It has a small stove which we bought, no dishwasher. Two bedrooms, each with double bed and closet. One bathroom straight ahead. And that's all there is, folks."

Janet spoke up, "Betty, you forgot our most recent addition: the folding card table and four chairs which are neatly put away somewhere."

The four women walked through the house. Each bedroom was big enough for a double bed with about two feet of space on each side and an unattached clothes closet in the corner by the door. Each had one of the card table chairs by the head of the bed. They looked around the kitchen and checked out the bathroom which had sink, a tub with shower, and a toilet.

Once they finished looking around, Betty said, "Let's put up the card table and chairs and get out the goodies." All agreed and in less than five minutes the four were at the table with the pill bag emptied on a plate. They all began teaching Patty what each pill was and what it was called and what it would do. "This one will relax you 'till you think you're drifting on clouds without a care in the world. This one will make you sleepy and two might make you feel numb and dumb. This one is the one you know, good old 'acid' as we call it. It can take you on a wild trip for several hours as you may have experienced. A 'bad trip' can also occur and be very frightening. You may see and hear and believe things and even do things that are totally different than the 'you' you know."

Patty watched her three companions and tried to follow the pattern of pills Joyce was taking. Janet and Betty were taking different ones. Before long everything became fuzzy and she had a hard time following Joyce. But she would take a pill every time Joyce did. They were her friends now and she was part of their circle. All would be well in this new world. She felt dazed and when she tried to get up to go to the bathroom she lost her balance and fell. She couldn't quite make it to her feet so she just peed where she lay. What the hell? Who cares? Piss on the world! And on the father who's a brute! And on the mother who was a wimp! She laughed, she sang, she slept, she woke, she was dancing with the parish priest, she was burning in hell, she was singing with the angels, Frank was crying at her feet and she peed on him. The sun was shining on the floor beside her when she came back from a night of dreams, weird phantasies and hallucinations. She was on the floor with open eyes and decided the girl sitting at the table might be Janet. She said a feeble, "Hi."

It was Janet who replied, "You're finally awake. You had quite a trip, apparently a very bad trip. It's one o'clock Sunday afternoon. Your friend Joyce is in bed with Betty. I'll check on them. If Joyce is going to take you home, you should get up and try to tidy yourself. You pissed your pants but they may be dry by now. I can loan you something to wear home if you need it."

The reality of the situation slowly became clear but it would dim and then return. She tried to force herself to connect with what was happening around her. She crawled up with the help of a chair and went into the bathroom. Her face was puffy and looked bruised. Her hair was in disarray. Her underwear and dress were dry but wrinkled and had the odor of urine. She decided she would go home as she was. What the hell difference did it make? It was her life. She had new friends. Screw her father.

It was about three o'clock when she left with Joyce to go home. Everyone hugged everyone and all agreed they had a bond and a need to maintain it. On the way home Patty and Joyce talked about the after-effects of the pills they took. Joyce said she was going to be more discriminating about pills and said it was not wise to take such an assortment. She said, "Betty will take anything available in drugs." Then she added, "She's also ready to take any female available for sex and she always makes herself available to me. But the drugs often lessen the satisfaction of a sexual encounter."

Patty raised the question, "Are you seriously thinking of moving in with them? And if you are, how soon do you think that might happen?"

Betty delayed answering for a few minutes. "I'm thinking about it but I'm not sure. I'm not sure of anything these days. Mom and Dad fight all the time and I expect them to split any day now. I couldn't go with Dad. He'd want me in his bed in no time. He's made a couple of passes which I told Mom about. And Mom is a nurse, works nights a lot, or at least says she is working. We don't share much. I think she knows I'm lesbian although she never mentions it. She's pretty hostile toward any girlfriends I bring home. I can't see any peace if I live with Mom, and I don't think she would care either way. They each pay half of my college expenses and Dad gives me $200 a month for personal needs. I could continue college and probably afford my share if I lived with Betty and Janet.

"But here we are at your house. I'll see you at the college in a few days. I would like to talk more about the whole situation. And I'd like to know more about your plans for the next few years."

As Patty walked toward the front door, the thought of facing her father surfaced. She had been *far far away*. She realized her thinking was still under the influence of the night of drugs and she was probably in no condition to confront her father. Jim was standing in the living room waiting. He watched her as she came in. Her disheveled appearance was obvious and her gait lacked its usual air of confidence.

Jim spoke, "This is the first time you have stayed out overnight without letting me know in advance. I believe we agreed a long time ago that wouldn't happen. Did you think I wouldn't worry or did you just not care? But never mind that now. You're a mess. You look like you haven't slept and I won't bother to ask you about drugs. I look at you and the answer is obvious. If you slept at all, it must have been in your clothes. They stink of urine. You know, you're a disgrace to me, to your mother, to the whole family, to this house. I'd be ashamed of you if one of your grandparents or an aunt or uncle came to visit. You talked about moving out. I think it's time. I'm through with you."

Patty's speech was a bit slurred but her cloudy mind understood her father's words. "Fine, Dad. I'll leave as soon as I can make arrangements and it won't be long. Then I'll be out of your life and you'll be out of mine forever."

Jim threw his hands in the air and walked away. Patty went to her room and got in bed. She tried to collect her thoughts about moving out and very soon a troubled, restless sleep took over.

The following morning Patty fixed herself some coffee and toast before she left for work. Her father was already gone. Kit was with her family on Sunday so she missed the father-daughter scene on Sunday. Kit came in the kitchen with a cheerful "Good Morning." Patty did not reply in kind but told Kit about the confrontation she had with her father. She said, "I'll be moving out soon, Kit, and I won't be coming back. I will miss seeing you and continuing to learn Spanish. When I get settled somewhere I'll get in touch with you and maybe we can get together occasionally."

Kit expressed regret that Patty would be leaving and added, "I know your father loves you but he has difficulty recognizing your independence. He worries about the danger of drug use and I can honestly say I do too. I know a lot of people who have serious problems with drugs and their lives are being ruined as a result. I hope that will never happen to you. You are an important person in my life and you always will be. You've been kind and encouraging and I'll always be grateful. By the way, I am planning to begin a course in American History at City College. It's a special course for those with limited English. You led me to it you know."

Patty thanked Kit for her comments and was off to the jewelry store. During the first few hours at work she had difficulty focusing on what she was doing. Her mind kept drifting to other things but then she couldn't remember what they were as she brought her attention back to her work. It was a difficult morning and the afternoon wasn't much better. The manager asked her several times if she was feeling all right. He obviously noticed the change.

When she finished the day she went to the nearby shop for coffee. She sat there for almost an hour trying to focus her jumbled thoughts. Her father's words, the night with Joyce and her friends, a plan to move, all interspersed with memories of the highs and lows of Saturday's drug party. This was a topsy-turvy world. She finally decided to walk home instead of taking the bus. She didn't get home until after seven. Jim and Kit had eaten. Patty found some food in the kitchen, took it to her room, and after eating she went to bed.

Tuesday was much like Monday only she was more aware of her poor performance at work and more focused on the need to make a change in her life. At the end of the day the manager said he would expect her on Saturday since the college semester was starting the next day. She had again agreed to work on Saturdays during the semester.

Earlier in the day she called Joyce and arranged to meet her for dinner at a nearby restaurant. Since each was considering a move the subject dominated their conversation. After a lengthy discussion of the pros and cons, they agreed they would like to move in with Janet and Betty. Joyce commented, "Betty and I will be happy to sleep together. I don't expect fidelity from her and she won't get it from me. But nonetheless we'll be bed-mates. You and Janet should hit it off okay. That's a pretty big bed so you could even manage with a 'no touching' rule."

Patty said, "How about going down to see them this coming Sunday? I have to work on Saturday. I'd like to take a look at their place again. And I'd like to do 'no drugs' this time."

Joyce responded, "You're always free to do drugs or not. I'll get some acid. I always do when I go there. Wonder how I'll manage when I live there. I can't stay high all the time. I'll give them a call and set it up for noon on Sunday. Do you want me to pick you up?"

Patty answered, "No, I'll take my own car. I don't know how soon you plan to move but I'd like to make the change one-day next week. I can't wait to get out of my house."

Joyce said she was thinking of a possible move day the next week. "I've packed some of my things already and my parents are aware I'm close to leaving. Not that they give a shit one way or the other."

On the way home Patty revisited their conversation and was satisfied with her decision and glad Joyce would be moving too. Joyce's being there would make it easier for her to get used to the other two women. She knew she said "no drugs" on Sunday but she couldn't help thinking "maybe one Pep Pill to celebrate my decision."

The rest of the week was uneventful but a bit of a blur. On Sunday afternoon the four young women were together in Haight-Ashbury. Everyone smoked some marijuana and everyone bought LSD for later. They walked through Janet and Betty's house again and examined the kitchen and cleaning supplies. They agreed on equal sharing of expenses and of keeping things reasonably neat and clean. Patty and Joyce could move in any time, just call a few hours in advance so Janet or Betty would be there.

Patty swallowed the LSD while they were doing the house tour. She decided she'd be home before "the trip" started. But before she arrived home she knew her heart rate was increasing and she began to have chills. Her house looked blue instead of white and all the trees turned yellow. She went directly to her room after shouting loudly "hello everyone" as she passed through the living room. She lay on her bed as her future danced in colored gowns and changing faces, everything beautiful and loving, stars shining everywhere and peace and love playing music in her ears. It was glorious and grand beyond imagination or belief. But there were scenes of strange places and persons, monsters evil and frightening. They floated in and out, far away, beside her, then inside her. She scratched at her stomach to get the demons out. The show went on and stopped and came back. She felt powerful and so alive she controlled the world. The demons inside her kept changing colors until they turned black and she began a troubled sleep.

It was past ten when she woke Monday morning. She found blood on her pajamas and sheets from the scratches she made in the night. She realized she missed her morning class but thought "to hell with it." She decided she would eat a little something and then get things ready for her move. Kit sat with her while she had a dish of cereal and orange juice. They talked about her moving and how much they meant to each other. She told Kit she was moving in with a couple of young women she recently met. She deliberately did not mention the names of her friends or where they would be living. She planned to disappear forever from her father's control.

Patty had no classes Wednesday afternoon. She went home, put her luggage in the car, said goodbye to Kit, and left for an uncertain future. She called earlier so she knew Betty would be expecting her at the Haight-Ashbury house. Betty greeted her with a warm hug and kiss on the mouth in welcome. Patty brought her luggage in and unpacked the clothes and toiletries she brought. Betty said she was expecting Joyce later in the day and suggested the four of them go out to dinner together to celebrate. Patty said, "I'm fine with the dinner and the celebration but I need to go light on the celebrating. I have an eight o'clock class in the morning."

About seven o'clock the four young women walked the eight blocks to Sam's Pizza Hut. They each had a couple of beers with dinner. As they left the Pizza Hut, Janet passed around "weed" to smoke on the way home. This was Patty's first marijuana. She didn't know what to expect. Before they reached the house she began to feel a pleasant euphoria and began laughing at every comment anyone made. The giddy feelings were soon replaced by anxiety. She became distrustful of her three companions and suspected their intentions toward her were evil. She thought, "This whole thing about moving to the house was a trick. The three of them are planning to harm me, possibly kill me, or hold me captive until my father pays ransom." She didn't know what to do. She finally said to her friends, "I want to get my car and go home. I'll pick up my things tomorrow."

When her friends laughed, it seemed like an evil laugh to Patty. She started to run but they grabbed her and tried to calm her. Joyce said, "It's the pot, Patty. You never smoked before and high grade can hit you pretty hard sometimes. No one here is going to hurt you. We have another block to go and we'll be home. You'll be able to lie down then and sleep it off." Her assurance calmed Patty enough to get her to the house.

As her three companions continued to chat, Patty got ready for bed, set her alarm for eight a.m. and crawled into bed. She could feel her heart racing and wondered if she'd be able to sleep. The night was more than fitful. There were frightening phantasies and strange dreams as she floated between sleep and troubled thoughts. When the alarm finally rang, she reached and turned it off. She was alone in bed so her bedmate must have left for class. She felt nauseous and hurried unsteadily to the bathroom. When she returned to her bed she was feeling dizzy and her thoughts were blurred. She went back to bed. Later in the day she found blankets on the living room sofa and decided her bedmate had slept there. That evening Janet told her, "I spent at least two hours off and on last night trying to comfort you and at times trying to control you. You kept calling Joan and Kit." Patty couldn't remember who Joan was. Later in the evening she remembered Joan was her maternal and favorite grandmother, the one who took care of her when Susan died.

It is difficult to know when Patty's life-course locked into a self-destructive pattern. Shutting off the alarm and deciding not to go to class didn't seem highly significant at the time. She missed two classes that morning, the same classes she missed on Monday. But Monday morning she overslept. There was no deliberate decision involved. This time she was awake and returned to bed after going to the bathroom. The decision came so easily, so readily. Of course she excused herself because she wasn't feeling well. She didn't consider why she wasn't feeling well; at least, she didn't consider it then. Months later in reviewing her life, she recalled the significance of that morning and saw it as a commitment to a life of addiction.

She went to one class on Friday and skipped the second one. "It's no big deal," she told herself. She smoked pot Friday evening and didn't get up to go to the jewelry store Saturday morning. Her downward course continued during the next several months. The following week she quit going to college without bothering to withdraw. She knew she would not return to McGregor Jewelry but didn't make the effort to let them know. She spent her days wandering the streets occasionally accompanied by Joyce or Betty. She hooked up with a couple of different guys, allowing physical intimacy but careful not to reveal any personal information. No matter how "lost" she got in the abuse of drugs, there was a firm and constant barrier preventing any reference to her prior life. The barrier was built of hatred for her father.

After three months without her, Patty's father began to regret his quarreling with her and lamented her loss. She left without a note or any information about where she was going. He quizzed Kit about Patty's leaving. She told him about their talk the day Patty left but could honestly say Patty had given her no information about her future nor had she heard anything from her.

Jim decided he had to find her and know she was alright. He went to City College and worked his way up through the hierarchy until he reached the president, Doctor Hawkins. No one was willing to give him any information since Patty was considered a responsible adult. Jim explained the situation although Doctor Hawkins seemed to be familiar with it, obviously from talking with other faculty. Jim said he was paying tuition and felt he should at least be able to get a minimum of information. Doctor Hawkins: "The records show the last class Patty attended was a Spanish class nine weeks ago. No one on our faculty has seen or heard from Patty since that last class. The finance office will not bill you for next semester and we'll evaluate the situation and possibly refund some of your payment for the present semester."

Jim replied, "I don't care about the money. Is there any way I can find out who her friends were? They might know something about where she is." Doctor Hawkins said he would inquire of her teachers and see what they might know about Patty's friends. If he discovered any helpful information, noting that it was unlikely, he would be in touch with Jim.

Three weeks later Jim had no news from Hawkins or Kit or friends from his office who knew Patty and whom he had asked to be on the lookout for her. He was unwilling to drop the matter. It became more important each day. He had a haunting feeling something bad may have happened or be happening to Patty. He had become lax about Sunday Mass but remembered how he and Susan had returned to Sunday Mass and to evening prayers when they were longing to have a child. They felt Patty might well have been an answer to their prayers. He was determined to go back to the former schedule of Sunday Mass and daily prayers. He remembered one of Susan's favorite expressions, "It won't hoit."

The following week he came up with another idea. The firm sometimes hired a private detective to find someone (for example, a missing husband) or watch someone (perhaps the husband before he went missing). He called the private detective, Jake, and asked him to come over. He told Jake the story of Patty's leaving home and the events before she left. He gave him information about Patty's car, make, model, year and license plate number. And he gave him Frank's name.

Before he left Jake asked if Patty ever mentioned Haight-Ashbury. Jim was familiar with the area due to articles in the papers and news on television. Jake said, "Young people are moving into that area in droves. It's becoming the drug capital of the country. Gays and lesbians are gathering there for the big 'coming out' in 1969. The '69' has become the symbol for homosexuality. Even the psychedelic promoter, Timothy Leary, is scheduled to come for the 'Summer of Love' next year. Long hair and minimal garb have become the norm. Drugs are sold on the street in plain sight. Police rarely enter the area and when they do, they are serenaded with continuous chanting: 'Turn on, tune in, drop out'. It's certainly an area I'll search. Do you have a recent picture of Patty?"

Jim said, "I have her high school graduation picture and she hasn't changed much since then, in appearance at least. I'll bring it in tomorrow if you'll stop by and pick it up. My secretary will have it if I'm in court or in conference."

Detective Jake picked up the picture the next day. Then he went first to his usual sources. He checked arrest records, speeding tickets, accident reports and hit and run reports. He looked at abandoned car records. He went by the college and talked to a couple of people he knew on the faculty. The Spanish teacher talked about Patty and said she was a good student and a nice person. She added, "There were some stories of drug use associated with her name and a friend of hers. I was completely surprised when Patty never showed up for another class." Jake left his card and asked the teacher to call him if she ever heard anything from or about Patty.

Jake thought to himself, "Haight-Ashbury is the most likely place for this girl to be. I need to walk around there a bit and check with some of the sellers. They tend to protect their customers but they're easily bought. And one can always hint about a tip to the police. Police are a threat to the small time solo-dealers." There would be a lot of sight-seers visiting Haight-Ashbury on Saturday and Sunday. Jake was looking for someone who might be living there. Better to go on a weekday, less crowded.

The four women were eating dinner one evening the following week. Betty and Patty typically prepared dinner because they were usually home all day or returned home in the early afternoon. The food varied a good deal depending on their level of sobriety more than their cooking abilities. During the meal Betty looked at Patty and said, "I have some news that might be of interest to you. I was making a small delivery to Phil today. Maybe you don't remember him. He's the guy selling pep pills and a few other goodies at his kiosk. Phil told me a sort of shabby looking man came up to him a couple of days ago and chatted a while about how interesting the area was becoming and how many new people seemed to be around. The guy took a picture out and said to Phil, 'I'm looking for this girl who's a good friend of mine.' As the guy showed Phil the picture, he said the girl wasn't really his girlfriend but she used to hang out with a group of six or seven people in the City College area. They all talked about coming to Haight-Ashbury and getting to know some people there. Phil thought the guy made a point of indicating the group's interest in finding a "supplier." Then he said, 'We haven't seen our friend in several weeks. Have you happened to see someone around who looks like this girl in the picture?' It was your picture he showed Phil, Patty.

"Phil said he thought you would want to know someone is looking for you. You've been a good customer and that's how he treats his customers. So there you have it. What do you make of it?"

Patty replied, "It's my father and he's hired a detective to find me. I need to disappear. Before I left home I told my father I never wanted to see him again and I meant it. I'll leave in the morning. I have no idea where to go but I'll probably head up the coast toward Oregon. I drove through that area a year ago when I went to Canada with a boyfriend whom I also never want to see again. I guess you three are the only ones I will ever want to see again."

Betty had more news. "Phil said you might be interested to know there's a town called Cave Junction in Southern Oregon where some of the people who hang out here are going. Phil has no idea what the attraction is other than it's a small town, not far from the coast and apparently does not have a very active or up-to-date police force. It seems there are outlets for 'the basic needs of happiness' as how Phil put it."

Patty responded, "Well, my friends, I think I'll pack up my stuff first thing in the morning and be on my way. Not likely my dad will find me in Cave Junction. I'm sorry to be leaving the three of you and I'll miss you. Anyone want to come along?"

Joyce said, "I might consider it later on. Keep in touch, who knows I may join you in a month or two." The four talked for a while about their lives and how time seems to go by so quickly. They agreed not one of them had any concrete plans for the future except Janet who said she is determined to continue her education long enough to be eligible for a secretarial position. And now Patty had an open ended plan to leave the area.

Before the evening was over each of her three friends assured Patty that her whereabouts would never be disclosed to anyone. Patty thanked them and said goodbye to Joyce and Betty who typically didn't get up until ten or eleven in the morning. She planned to leave by eight a.m. and would see Janet before leaving. She began getting her things together before she went to bed.

Patty ate an early breakfast, finished her packing, said goodbye to Janet and was on her way before eight o'clock. She looked at her maps and checked the costal route. It was about 400 miles to Cave Junction, a long drive but she had an early start. She was grateful her mind was clear this morning and recalled she fortunately abstained from drug use the previous day.

After about thirty minutes of driving she became reflective. She felt proud she made this decision; there was a plan in her mind, a purpose in her actions, something definite to do this day. It had been months since a single day was noteworthy. One day just drifted into another, going nowhere. They were all the same, relatively meaningless. Time had truly become insignificant. Pot, psychedelics, and more recently heroin certainly brought some remarkable highs but, as she thought about it, not much else except that dark feeling of a deep need, always for more. Her mental meanderings eventually led to the jewelry shop. She enjoyed that work and the people who worked there. Why did she quit? She didn't quit; she just didn't go back. It was the same thing with school. There were no real decisions. She decided there was just "neglect."

It was time for a break. She stopped at the first sign for food, got coffee and a doughnut, and used the restroom. When she was on the road again, her reflections returned. She had just made another decision, the decision to stop and do what she did. She went through each separate step and felt like complimenting herself. It felt good to make even little decisions and to carry them out. "Why does that seem so unusual?" she pondered. She had no one to talk to, no one to please, no one with expectations. She was *free* and could decide and do whatever she decided. Was life really that simple?

After another three hours on the road she stopped for toilet, lunch and gas in that order. Back in the car she assumed she would be in Cave Junction by dinner time. Her mind drifted back to the mental wanderings of the morning. There was something sobering about them. She smiled as the word "sobering" came to mind. She said to the empty car, "How many times have I said to myself in the midst and mist of a 'trip', I never want to be sober again." But the thought of "a sober world" momentarily attracted her and "turned her on and tuned her in" to her childhood years, to Kit, to Grandmother Joan, the Madames, the Jesuits, the jewelry shop. Alongside those came a "somber world" of a dying mother, a detached father, an unfaithful Frank, a failed employee and a failed student. Again to the empty car, "Where the hell is my life going?"

The sun was still above the horizon when she drove into Cave Junction. "Not much of a town," she said to herself, and then added, "Be careful about all this talking to yourself. You can get locked up for symptoms like that." The highway went through the center of town. It appeared she must choose one of the two motels. She chose the second, the Sleep Inn which was across the street from Mac's Diner.

Since she moved to Haight-Ashbury she always kept $400 in traveler's checks available in her belongings. These and about $200 cash would have to do her until she could find a bank and get her money transferred from San Francisco. She would then have a total of about three thousand dollars. She rented a room, brought her bags in from the car, and decided to stretch her legs in a fifteen-minute walk before it got dark. She walked toward the mountains northeast of the motel. After she walked a short time the houses thinned out and large gardens appeared with farm-houses not far away. She turned left on the last street and as she walked she noted two or three groups of six to eight young people, long haired males, scantily clad females "hanging out" and almost certainly smoking marijuana. The thought crossed her mind to "make a buy." She was carrying too much cash and was a stranger to the area. Not a safe thing to do. But now she knew where there was a "watering hole"; and she hadn't even unpacked her bags. Where there was "weed", there would be a "garden". She took another left back to the highway. Again left and in a short time she was back at the motel. She ate a steak dinner at Mac's, returned to the motel, unpacked her bag and went to bed.

Sleep came quickly but was troubled. She kept dreaming and waking with fear. Frank was driving, high on crack and out to show the world how fast he could go. The speedometer read ninety and there was a sharp curve ahead. She woke in fear. She was in her room at home and her father came in carrying her dead mother and threw her on the floor in front of Patty. She woke in fear. She was in the jewelry shop and the manager was choking her and screaming obscenities. She woke in fear. She was fully awake before eight a.m. and feeling terrible. Before getting out of bed, she decided breakfast held no interest for her. She needed something to get herself in gear and decided some coke would do the trick.

She got dressed and took some fives and tens and left for the area she spotted the night before. Sure enough there were six users standing together smoking pot. As she approached and was a few steps away she quietly said, "Anyone have a little coke? I just got in town last night and I'm having a bad morning."

One of the guys replied, "I can help you, doll. You want to trade for sex or you got some cash? Another time I might not accept the cash but you're looking pretty needy and a little seedy so your body may not be fully tuned yet. Next time it will be sex only, no cash. I want to have some of that sugar you're carrying around."

Patty gave him the money for two small packs of powdered cocaine. As she walked away she decided she couldn't wait to get back to the motel so she opened one pack carefully, licked her finger, put her finger in the pack and rubbed the powder on her gums. She'd sniff some of the remainder when she got to the motel. Within a few minutes she felt happier and energetic. *Now* she would like some breakfast. She stopped at a little café for coffee and pancakes. The young girl serving her seemed unfriendly and by the time Patty left the café she suspected the girl called someone to report Patty's presence.

She continued the paranoid feelings when she got to the motel and for a time considered leaving Cave Junction and driving on to Grants Pass, a larger town and more inland. She snorted the rest of the crack and enjoyed the euphoria, but within two hours it was gone. One pack used to do her. Today two packs aren't doing the trick. She thought of going back to the supplier and getting three or four packs but she remembered his terms and decided sex with that creep was more than she could tolerate. She just lay on her bed in a listless almost numb state until past noon.

Her mind came back to the possibility of leaving Cave Junction. She decided it might be good to check on employment opportunities before leaving. She went to the desk at the motel and asked about work in the area. The woman replied, "Things are picking up a little, Honey. During summer months we have more tourists stopping for two or three days to look at the Oregon Caves. There's also river rafting and tubing close by. The Siskiyou Smokejumper Base is a few miles from here and is an interesting place. We've had some forest fires in the past that nearly wiped out the town.

"You might find a job at one of the cafes in town or the Dry Goods store a few blocks west on the road you came in on. In another week I'll be looking for someone to take the evening shift here at the desk. My house is in back of the motel. You can have a room in my house and use the kitchen if you take the job. But I need to be clear with you, Honey; it doesn't pay much and would only be for July and August."

Patty said, "Can I think it over for a couple of days? It sounds like it might be a good fit for me. Will you hold it open for two days?"

The reply, "I sure will, Honey. You look like a reliable person. Let me know when you make up your mind. I'm Mary by the way. I'll look forward to seeing you again." Patty wasn't sure she wanted to stay long in Cave Junction. She remembered her friend Betty suggested a lot of people were leaving Haight-Ashbury and moving here. She said to herself, "I guess they're still on the way."

Patty walked up and back along the few blocks facing the highway. It was the commercial part of town. There were three cafes, a small grocery store and the General Store with sundries: a broad variety of household items, personal items, a few tools and so forth. There was a small movie theater. A total of about twenty people could be seen on the streets. The guy who sold her the coke walked out from a side street. He cheerfully spoke. "Hello, little doll. How's about a business exchange? A little lovin' will get you two packs, one before the hump and one after. Two packs are more than I usually do but it's early in the day and you're fresh meat."

Patty's immediate desire was to "get some coke," whatever the cost. Mention of it raised the need for the first time this morning. But a few other thoughts flashed through Patty's mind. "This creep is insulting. He thinks I'm some coke-head slut passing through town and ready to trade a piece of my ass for his coke." Was it the small town atmosphere that made her view things differently this morning? Was it the woman at the motel who seemed so friendly and accepting of her? This was not just a few hundred miles from San Francisco. It wasn't Haight-Ashbury where everybody was really a nobody. For some strange reason she felt she was losing her anonymity here even though she was a total stranger in town. She said, "Fuck off," and walked away.

Patty decided to take a drive somewhere back on the coastal highway. She checked the maps and decided to go north toward Gold Beach about fifty miles away. It felt good to be off by herself again and that realization was something of a revelation. She recalled how *present* others had always been in her life. She was never alone unless she was driving or sleeping. She was so accustomed to having others around it felt strange to be by herself. There were no demands, no expectations from anyone. For the first time in her life she felt free. Her reflections continued as she reached highway 101 and drove north. Right after the thought of freedom came the self-question, "Are you as free as you think you are? Can you honestly say you're free when you still respond to that internal gnawing for acid or coke or weed, or whatever's available to quell that overwhelming urge? If that jerk this morning had not been so crude, would you have accepted his offer?" Patty's reflections were sobering. She diverted her attention to the ocean view.

As she drove into Gold Beach she felt hungry. She passed several motels and two or three restaurants. When she reached the center of town she drove to a side street, parked and walked back to a restaurant she noticed on Main Street, a restaurant with the Chinese food she loved. After lunch she walked to the park near the wharf, sat on a bench and studied the beauty of the area. "This is too good to be true; I feel so relaxed," she said to herself. She blissfully wandered along the beach area for over two hours and then decided it was time to go back to Cave Junction. Before she left she went to the local bank and opened an account transferring the money from her San Francisco account. Cave Junction was too small to have a bank.

On the way home she kept thinking about Mary and her offer of the motel job. She said, "Mary is a likeable person and probably easy to be with. She doesn't appear to be a busy-body which is an asset. I don't want anyone prying into my affairs. The job is only for two months beginning July first, next Thursday. That would give me some time to consider whether I want to stay here permanently or consider something more like Gold Beach. Cave Junction may become too small for me after a couple of months."

She watched television in her room during the evening hours and then had a restless sleep, again with frightening dreams. While having breakfast the following morning she decided to take the motel job. Mary responded to the bell in the back room when Patty opened the office door. "Good morning, Mary. I've thought about it enough. I decided I would like to take the job, but before we agree perhaps you should tell me the particulars."

Mary seemed pleased and responded, "That makes it a good morning for me, Honey. Let's have a look in the back room here or 'the office' as I call it. Then I'll show you my house and the room available there." The back room had a small table with two chairs, a sink, and a small refrigerator and a toaster on a counter. There was a little wall-cabinet with a few dishes. There was one arm chair and a sleep-sofa and a separate bathroom. Mary explained, "When someone opens the door to the front desk, the bell rings in here. So if you're napping or just sitting in here you'll know when someone comes in at the desk."

Mary took Patty out the back door of the office. "Let's have a look at my house. I had no reason to mention it before, but I live with my husband. He's confined to a wheel chair by day and has been for the past five years. We were exploring the Caves together. It was a cold day and moisture accumulates inside the Caves. Albert stepped on a rock that was iced. He fell and fractured two vertebrae that required surgery. He hasn't walked since that day. He gets around in his wheel chair and takes care of his needs. I help him into bed at night and out in the morning. In spite of it all, he's high spirited with a good sense of humor. His pain is pretty well relieved by the codeine he takes and which I monitor for him."

The house was about twenty yards from the office door. When Mary opened the house door, she called, "Albert, I have a visitor with me. Don't want to surprise you." They walked into the living room and found Albert reading a book. Mary said, "Albert dear, this is Patty the girl I mentioned to you the other day, the girl I asked to help me in the office. She is considering taking the job and we're just looking around. If she takes the job, Patty will have a room here with us and will have 'kitchen privileges.' She will use the bedroom in the back of the house, the one with the sink, toilet and shower."

Albert smiled and reached out his hand to Patty, saying, "Welcome, welcome. It's a pleasure to meet you. Mary told me you were a pretty young lady and she sure got that right. It would be nice to have a third party in the house to settle all the arguments Mary and I have" said with a big smile and a wink.

Patty replied, "Thanks for your welcome. I think Mary and I will get along well together so you should be prepared to lose some arguments. I'm likely to favor my boss." Albert chuckled.

Mary said, "We'll move along so I can get back to the office. I'll show you your room and bathroom, Patty, and then we'll look at the kitchen." The bedroom and bath looked fine to Patty. They moved on to the kitchen. It was well equipped and had all the modern conveniences. Mary showed

Patty a shelf in the refrigerator that would be hers and also her shelf in one of the cabinets. When the cabinet door was open Mary pointed to the shelf below Patty's and said, "This is Albert's OxyContin. Thought I should tell you so you don't think it's aspirin or something." Patty hoped her thoughts didn't show on her face.

Mary called to Albert, "We're going back to the office to talk and go over the job details." Albert called a goodbye to Patty who responded with, "Nice to have met you. See you again."

Mary and Patty sat down together at the office desk. Mary explained that most people who will be coming during the next two months are regular customers and will have reservations made in advance. She added, "There may be two or three additional rooms available most days of the week." Mary continued, "I would like you to work from three to ten p.m. Monday through Friday. Those with reservations are asked to check in prior to seven p.m. We normally close the office at ten p.m. Travelers coming through here rarely stop in town after dark. Cave Junction is hardly a welcoming town at night. The town shops close by seven or eight at the latest. Even the movie has the last show at six. The only ones still moving around town later are the hoodlums and druggies. And we have an increasing number of those. They're part of the reason the town shuts down like it does.

"In addition to the hours I mentioned I'll ask you to cover the office from nine a.m. until noon Sunday mornings. We're Catholic, and Albert and I go to ten o'clock Mass in Gold Beach. It's really the only outing the poor man has on a regular basis. So those are the hours. I can only pay you four dollars an hour for the thirty-eight hours on your schedule. Pay day is every Saturday. If I ask you to work overtime it will be six dollars an hour. I know that's not much but jobs are scarce around here and the motel doesn't do well after the season. Actually we've thought of closing from October first to the first of May but we have no place to go during that time and we'd get so lonely. We have no family and no one we're really close to. Even one or two customers a week livens up our life a little, at least my life. Doesn't do much for Albert except it gives us something to talk about.

"We only have sixteen rooms, two single beds in each. A local woman cleans the rooms each morning and changes linens for new customers. I think that covers everything. You can think it over some more if you'd like but a local high school student asked me about 'work' and I told her to check with me day after tomorrow."

Patty's decision was made. "Everything you showed me and talked about sounds fine to me. I'll take it, Mary. I'll pay you my room rent through next Wednesday and then I'll move into your house and be on your time-clock."

As Patty left she began wondering what to do with the few days before the job started. Thoughts of her prior employment came back and flooded her mind with the foolhardy way in which she lived those last few months in San Francisco. Mentally she sorted through the debris of the life she left behind. Her mind flashed back to those she now blamed for her behavior. There was her tyrannical father, her neglectful and eventually crazed mother. There was Frank the phony, full of lies and deceit. There was Joyce, her classmate, who turned against her and paired with Betty, the lesbian housemate. She summarized her thinking in words as she entered her room, "All those people let me down when I needed them."

The spoken words sounded hollow to her. Then she remembered the words of a Jesuit teacher at St. Thomas Academy, "If you find yourself making excuses for your behavior, look carefully at the behavior. Ask yourself, 'Why are excuses necessary?'" The answer was clear. There was no excuse; there was a reason.

Acid, pot, coke in whatever form she could find them: these were the reason, these are still the reason. "Those you can't blame on anyone," she said out loud. Patty lay on her bed for half an hour contemplating the truth of her situation. She dozed for a while and when she woke her thoughts were on the job and preparations she needed to make.

Patty decided to have a look at the local market where she will be buying her groceries. She wanted some idea of what was available. As she left the market a young girl, maybe fourteen or fifteen years old, walked beside her and quietly said, "Are you looking to buy?" Then the girl kept talking about the nice weather, the quiet of the town, how far it was to the ocean, and various sights in the area. Her comments were a deliberate distraction to Patty and kept her 'off balance' in her resolve. At the same time the girl's very presence and the offer she made stirred the memories of "highs" and "trips" and "bliss" from the past. Patty wasn't thinking; she was caught in a "stash" of memories that unwittingly spilled over into words, "What you got?"

They reached a side street. The dealer said, "Let's turn here. The guy in the car in the next block has everything you could want. We can give you two 'window panes' of acid, a small pack of weed, and four caps of coke for twenty-five dollars. That's a bargain price for the pack. We make it up in advance. It's a good seller. If you got the cash, I'll signal him and the pack will be ready when we reach the car. Pretend you're asking for directions. Make the exchange with the driver while I get in the car and then we'll drive away."

As Patty looked back on the transaction she was aware of how easily and methodically it went. What a smooth operation! They've sold drugs in places other than Haight-Ashbury, places where police are on the lookout. Or maybe they're just practicing the routine for the big time somewhere else. Patty checked the bag in anticipation of where this could take her over the next few days. She labeled the whole event "a celebration" before beginning her new job. She wasn't up to expressing the parallel thought, "How easily I succumb to drugs."

The celebration began as soon as Patty reached her motel room. She knew the coke would act the fastest, as she opened a pack and rubbed it on her gums. In minutes the euphoria lifted her mood and quickened her thinking. Now there was the need to maintain her high so acid was chosen not only to enhance but to prolong the effects. Patty spent the next five days lost in a world of highs and lows, all driven by the choice and timing and layering of drugs. The "highs" were elevations to another world of peace and love, indescribable in words, beyond ecstasy, beyond bliss. And the "lows" brought nightmares, debilitating paranoia, hallucinatory periods and frightening reality.

In spite of her lengthy estrangement from reality, Patty knew when it was Wednesday and tomorrow would be her first work day. She had carefully planned to extract the "max" from the drugs. She smoked her last marijuana Tuesday evening. This was 'sober-up' day. She slept poorly during the night and was nauseous on waking. In the mirror she saw her blood shot eyes, her sallow cheeks, her matted hair and over-all a sickly look. For a moment the thought, "I'll tell Mary I'm sick and unable to work." But there came a quick rebuttal from somewhere inside her, "Not this time, Chickie. You work tomorrow. Now get ready."

She felt unsteady as she walked to the nearest spot for breakfast, food that only increased her nausea. She drank her coffee and returned to her room. She packed her clothes and personal items and took them with her to the office where Mary was waiting. She was greeted with, "Good morning, Honey. I haven't seen much of you these past days. I wondered if you were away but your car was always here. Are you feeling well? Have you been ill? You don't look too good, Honey."

Patty responded, "I've had some difficulties these past few days and am not feeling too chipper this morning. But I'll manage okay. I'd like to get settled in my room in your house and I'll show up here by three p.m." Patty knew she was feeling worse than she looked and worse than she sounded. What she really needed was some coke and she'd be on top of the world. Mary gave her a key to the house and told her to go on over. Al was expecting her.

Patty entered the house quietly hoping not to engage Albert. She went in her room and quickly closed the door. She lay on the bed hoping to relieve the increasing nausea and tremors. She could feel her heart racing and when she tried to stand vertigo was severe. She couldn't get comfortable on the bed and she was afraid to stand. There were only a few hours before her shift was to begin. After an hour that seemed like a few minutes she got up carefully and slowly and managed to unpack her clothes and the few belongings she brought. Although she had no appetite for food she knew she had to go to the grocery store before her shift began because it would be closed before her shift ended.

Patty left quietly without arousing Albert. She felt unsteady but managed to walk to her car. The fresh air and the movement gave her more confidence if not more comfort. She drove carefully to the store and returned with two bags of groceries. When she entered the house, Albert was in the living room and spoke, "It's good to see you again, Honey. I hope you don't mind me calling you that. It's what Mary always calls you. I think she's pretty fond of you. You know the space you have for your groceries in the fridge and the closet. Just help yourself."

Patty tried to muster some enthusiasm as she replied, "Thanks, Albert. I appreciate the room and the welcome you are both providing me. I'll put my groceries away and then get ready for my first shift." Before Patty got to the kitchen her mind flashed on the shelf just below her shelf. OxyContin! Waiting to be had! As she put her groceries on the shelf, she kept her back to the living room doorway. She took the OxyContin bottle and opened it. "There must be twenty or more. She won't miss two," she told herself as she put two in her pocket.

She left the kitchen and went quickly to her room to put on some makeup, change her blouse and prepare for the job. She went in her bathroom, put water in the glass and reached in her pocket. She was putting the first pill in her mouth. She stopped. Was it a voice she heard? Whose voice? Was it the nun who gave her such a hard time in eighth grade? Was it her father's voice? Was it Kit's? Was it her own voice? Was there really a voice? "Stealing destroys integrity!" It struck a sensitive chord. As Patty left the house she went by the kitchen and replaced the two OxyContin. It was ten minutes to three. She went to the office to relieve Mary.

Later on she realized she made one of many recurring decisions when she was in the kitchen; decisions with which she struggled over the coming weeks. The desire for drugs didn't go away nor did it come and go as some desires do. It was constant. It seemed there was never a moment that "need" was absent. Sometimes it seemed to fill her totally and there was no room for food or work or sleep or life itself. There were off-duty times when the decision included "do not leave the house." She would talk with Albert and get him to tell stories about his life and theirs. He would ask her about her life; but she was reluctant to give him any information. His questions easily set off those feelings of paranoia which she recognized as intermittent from her prior use of drugs.

One day to fill her morning hours Patty began looking through books in the living room bookcase. It felt like years since she read a good book. There was a Bible and a number of religious books. One day she picked up C.S. Lewis' *The Screwtape Letters*. She was immediately intrigued. It seemed so relevant to her situation. Drug dealers personified Wormwood only they were more successful in corrupting their victims and securing their damnation. The arguments submitted by Screwtape were readily comprehensible to her. When she finished that book, she began Lewis' *The Problem of Pain*.

The reading not only captured her thinking but soothed her restlessness. Tremors temporarily stopped. Her pulse rate slowed. There was a feeling of calm. Headaches were lessened. But when she was at the front desk, the *other world* came pouring back in. Her speech was hesitant, her decisions uncertain, her hands shaky. Her suspicions about some of the motel guests boarded on paranoia. At night she often had chills and sleep continued to come in short spans of about thirty minutes. And waking periods focused more and more on ghosts of the past. Patty had faded memories of early warmth and love from her mother. But those scenes were always shattered by memories of her mother's withdrawal from the table, from the family, from life. She remembered thinking her mother caused her own death to get away from Patty. "Why not, she got away from me in every other way," she said to herself. After her mother died, the name *Susan* was never spoken even when family or friends visited. It was her father's decision. Kit, like everyone else, always referred to "your mother" without using the name.

In times of semi-wakefulness, the ghost of her father roamed through her thoughts with him looking angry, sullen, uncaring. He was always lecturing her and she would put her fingers in her ears so she couldn't hear him. She was afraid of him even in these reveries and it was all she could do not to cry out or run out of her room. Patty knew these thoughts were too vivid and too real to be sane. Then she'd realized "my mind has not recovered from my drug use."

When morning came and she was out of bed and moving about she understood all these reviews of her childhood were not totally accurate but were exaggerated feelings from the past. She became increasingly aware that past drug use left its mark on her mind and she would just have to cope with this mental turmoil until it stopped.

In order to feed her need for mental relief Patty went back to C.S. Lewis and *Surprised by Joy*. Lewis's books brought her mind back to the faith of her early life, faith supported by her parents and family, by the Madames of the Sacred Heart and by the Jesuits. But consolation in these thoughts was short lived, for then she faced the host of sins of her last several years. She summed it all up saying, "No wonder God has abandoned me." She tried to pray but couldn't remember the words she knew so well. Searching for words only brought more confusion and depressed feelings.

The time at work became more difficult for Patty. She became easily confused over the names of guests and had trouble remembering even the simple things she needed to do to help them feel welcome and comfortable. By mid-August she dreaded each day's work. She felt sad and lonely and spent little time in the presence of Mary and Albert. She knew it was noticeable to them so she tried to act cheerful in their presence. Occasionally, Mary would gently say, "Are you feeling okay, Honey?"

By the last week of August, she could hardly drag herself out of bed by noon. She dreaded each day. She cried easily when there was any kind of problem in the office. She always assumed it was her fault. Sometimes she just didn't care and other times she brooded for hours about some insignificant thing. She wanted so badly for the month to end. At the same time, she felt desperate about the future. She had no plans, very little money left, and no friends other than Mary and Albert. She had money enough to rent a room again for a few days. It was reaching a point where sex for drugs was the only way to go back to a life she had vowed to end.

Patty went to the office about ten to three on her last working day. When she came in, Mary said, "Let's go in the back room for a few minutes I want to talk to you." After they both sat down, Mary continued, "I know you haven't been feeling your usual self, Honey, for the last three or four weeks. If you'll pardon an interfering old lady, I believe you have not been well. If there's nothing physically wrong, then I suspect you've become quite depressed. You have been careful not to talk about your past so I really don't know anything about you. But I suspect there is some great sadness or disappointment in your life that you are carrying around like a bag of stale garbage that only weighs you down and makes everything seem rotten. The word in the street (people tell me all kinds of things when I'm out shopping) is, 'You're a druggy.' Now if that's true, I've seen no evidence of drug use since you began working for me. I deliberately told you about Albert's OxyContin to test you. I've occasionally checked on how many pills were there. You've never taken one. But if you were a druggy, the other possibility for your poor health is withdrawal. That's a tough road Albert and I have been down. We had Albert's nephew live with us for a year when he came off drugs. It was not easy for us but it was worse for him. Tell me what's wrong, Honey, if you can and if you will."

The dam broke and Patty's tears flowed freely for several minutes. Mary filled the space with her kindness. "Honey, you don't need to leave the house tomorrow. Stay with us until you're feeling better. You're in no condition to be driving off somewhere and there is no work in the area right now. Stay here. If you want to, you can take a shift once in a while when you feel up to it. Things will be pretty light around here. Let us be a little help to you until things are brighter. You will be a blessing in our lives."

Patty continued weeping as Mary spoke. She wiped her eyes and spoke haltingly, "Thank you, Mary, for being so open with me and so kind and gentle. Yes, I don't feel well and I'm sure my physical ails result from prior drug use. And I am horribly depressed. I would like to see a psychiatrist but I can't afford it and I'm not sure it would help."

Mary replied, "I don't think we could help you with a psychiatrist's fees and there are no psychiatrists in this area. There is a "counselor" at our church but I don't know how helpful she might be. You could apply for medical assistance, Honey, now that you will be unemployed and you have an illness that needs care. There is information about medical assistance at the post office and I think they have government applications there. I'm not sure, but you could ask. In the meantime, you just keep your room at our house and living here will just continue as it is now. If you need some help with groceries, let us know."

Patty said, "I have money enough to carry me for several weeks or even months if I'm not paying rent or trying to travel. I can't but wonder why you and Albert are so willing to help me. You have been kind since the first day I met you and I can honestly say I think your kindness encouraged me to try to make some changes in my life. I truly needed someone to reach out to me with the gentleness you have shown. No matter what happens in my life, you both have been a blessing I will never forget. There's the bell. I'll go out to the desk and take care of it."

As the two women stood, Mary put her arms around Patty and as she pulled her close she could feel her sobbing again. Patty delayed a short time and dried her eyes; then she went to the desk to care for a guest who was checking out.

When her shift ended that evening Patty went to the house and found Mary and Albert waiting up for her. They were usually asleep by the time Patty came home. Mary had made a key lime pie which she knew was Patty's favorite. They toasted Patty with ginger ale and welcomed her as their new house guest. Patty thanked them for their kindness and generosity and said, "I will always remember you with love in my heart."

After the party ended Patty went to her room thinking, "There must be someone else I remember with love. Kit comes to mind and my maternal grandmother, Joan, whom I haven't thought of for months or even years. It's remarkable how drug use walled off even the memories of the good things and of the good people in my life." In spite of the display of affection from Mary and Albert and a reprieve from driving down the road to nowhere, sleep came intermittently with the same half-awake periods and their haunting scenes from the past, misshapen by paranoia and depression. It was a troubled night.

The following day Patty went to the Post Office and obtained an application for Social Security Disability. She read through the instructions on "who should apply." It included "persons recovering from substance abuse" and in another section "persons with depression." She completed the application and put it in the mail before leaving the post office.

Late the following week Patty received a notice from Social Security informing her that her application had been received. It instructed her to contact Stephen Moke, M.D. in Grants Pass, Oregon and request an evaluation regarding eligibility. She phoned Dr. Moke that afternoon and obtained an appointment for the following Monday at two p.m.

Patty told Mary and Albert about the application and about having an appointment to see a physician to evaluate her need for Social Security benefits. Albert was the first to respond, "We're pleased you've gone ahead with this, Patty. It's gratifying to us to witness your obvious desire to take charge of your life and to take some steps to do so. Nice going, Honey!"

Mary was more effusive, "Oh, Honey, I'm so happy for you. This is the beginning of your return to the person you were before you got caught up in the drug world. We believe in your goodness and we pray together each night that you will find your way back to a world of peace and health and love. If you want, we would be happy to take you to your appointment."

Patty replied, "Thank you both. Your kindness has made this possible. What you have done, taking me into your home and treating me like I'm your daughter, has been a blessing for me and motivates me to try to improve my life. I will be forever grateful.

"And thanks for the offer of a ride to Grants Pass. I've checked my maps and it looks like an easy drive, about thirty miles. I'll be fine." Moments like these cheered Patty, but never for long. They were like a momentary shaft of sunlight breaking through a dark, threatening, ever-present sense of gloom.

After the usual erratic night, Patty had a late breakfast Monday morning and then prepared to leave for Grants Pass. Mary brought Albert out to the car and they both waved goodbye as she drove away. She arrived in Grants Pass about noon. She found the doctor's office and then drove to the business area of town to spend some time before her appointment. She saw signs for the Rogue River Park. She drove there and walked around for half an hour reflecting on the recent twists and turns of life that brought her to this place at this time. She was pleasantly surprised to realize she hadn't even thought of looking for "a buy" when she drove into town. She bought coffee and a turkey sandwich at a nearby stand and sat on a bench wondering what questions the psychiatrist would ask.

She arrived at Doctor Moke's office about ten to two. Inside the waiting room there was another door with a sign, "Doctor Moke is in session. He will be with you shortly." There was also a door marked "Bathrooms." That was good to know she thought. Patty sat in one of the arm chairs and picked up the Daily Courier on the table beside her. She glanced through it as her thoughts listlessly came and went. Before long the door marked

Steve Moke, M.D. opened and closed after an older man walked out and then exited the building. As the clock in the room chimed two the doctor's door opened again. A slim man of medium height stepped out and said, "Ms. Patricia Watson." As Patty stood in response, the doctor introduced himself and motioned for her to come in.

There was a leather top desk with a swivel arm chair behind it and two arm chairs facing it. Dr. Moke motioned for Patty to sit in an arm chair. She noted some tasteful art pictures decorated the walls. The doctor spoke, "You are here for a Social Security evaluation based on information you recently sent to that agency. I do not get a copy of your application but I am asked to examine your mental health and report my findings to the Social Security Office. On the basis of my report they will determine whether or not you are eligible for Social Security health care. So I will need to ask you questions about your past and current life. These questions will also relate to your life as a child and will include questions about other significant family members. My questions will intrude into your personal and private world. Your answers to me are confidential and will not be revealed to anyone else including the Social Security Office. They will receive only my conclusions about your health, not the information you give me to reach those conclusions. Is all of that clear and do you have any questions for me?"

Patty understood what the doctor said, was pleased with his openness and felt comfortable with him. She asked, "What if there are things I don't remember?"

He replied, "If you don't remember something I ask about, simply say, 'I don't remember.' As we move along in your story you may remember something you thought you had forgotten. If the memory shows up later, I would expect you to let me know. That sort of thing happens quite frequently once we start talking. And feel free to ask me questions if you don't understand what I'm asking. This meeting will last between an hour and a half and two hours. If that's tiring and you'd like a break let me know and we'll stop for five minutes or so. Or if you want to use the lady's room any time let me know. You probably saw the door when you came into the waiting room. By the way, would you like a glass of water, a coke or ginger ale? I have a fridge through that door marked Private." Patty shook her head as he asked about something to drink. "Okay then, are we good to go?" Patty nodded in answer. He added, "If you do need a break, please, interrupt me, raise your hand, holler, whatever it takes. I get going sometimes with my questions and don't know when to stop. But I will try to watch the time."

As Doctor Moke talked, Patty found herself feeling more and more at ease and increasingly comfortable with him. The questions began and Patty found herself confronting areas of her life which she hadn't thought about in years. They reviewed memories of her childhood and how those memories changed from happy to sad to angry and to an increasing sense of isolation. Her mother's illness took on new dimensions as Patty came up with bits and pieces in a collage of feelings. The family's response to her mother's death left a stark view of that time. Memories of Patty's educational years were for the most part positive but the experience was overshadowed by the associated conflict with her father. Their relationship dominated not just her teen years but her whole life, a fact which surfaced in the interview but which Dr. Moke mentally noted was viewed very narrowly by Patty.

After an hour passed, Dr. Moke suggested they take a break. He commented, "Ms. Watson, you are doing very well. Your memories are rusty perhaps and some may have been lost over time, but your mind seems willing to do the search. Can I bring you a coke? I think I'll have one." Patty nodded in response. Her mouth was feeling dry from talking so much. She wondered when she ever sat for one hour and talked to the same person. "Probably never" was the answer.

When they started again Dr. Moke asked about friends in school and relationships with teachers, those she liked and those she didn't like. Then came boyfriends and she summarized her one love affair and how it ended with Frank. Moke probed that story a bit. Then he moved to employment and for the first time he caught a feeling of enthusiasm. But once more the story ended sadly and was coupled with the subject of drugs in this overview of Patty's life. The time in Haight-Ashbury was covered briefly, the friends, the drugs, the path downward. There was no need to dwell on specifics; Moke's attitude was "increased desire always accompanies details in this area."

Next the interview moved to the last several months in Cave Junction and covered the struggle with drugs and the growing symptoms associated with their discontinuance. Evidence of depression was obvious in her current and recent moods, poor sleep patterns, problems with memory, lack of interest, and morbid focus. Her past was prelude to depression when one considered the tragic childhood events, the faulty adult responses to her needs, the severe family disruption in her teen years apparently related to an emotionally struggling father.

When they completed the evaluation session, Dr. Moke told Patty he would send his report to the Social Security office by the next day. He said he would recommend she be given Social Security coverage until her condition returned to normal. He added, "If you do receive coverage, it may well be in effect for a limited period. It's also possible you may not have a decision from their office for two or three months."

Patty thanked Doctor Moke for his time saying, "I was surprised how easy it was to talk to you and how many things came back to me as we talked. Your questions and our exchange seemed to open up so many areas that I need to look at more closely. Thank you for your time and your kindness. It was helpful."

Patty's comments aided Doctor Moke in making a decision he began to consider during the interview. He said, "It is evident from our talk you would be a good candidate for a few weeks of psychiatric care. I think you would benefit greatly from treatment. Would you consider coming as my patient for a short time?"

Patty responded quickly, "I wish I could, but unfortunately my funds are nearly exhausted. I'm too scattered and too lame-brained even to try to find a job right now. If things improve and I can find work, I would like to come and have some sessions with you."

The doctor replied, "I've been quite impressed by your responsiveness today and I believe you would respond well to a short period of care. Your earlier life was limiting for you and not because of your fault or anyone's fault. There were events over which no one had control, for example, the untimely death of your mother when others responded to their own lives, their own needs, in their own ways, and you got lost in the shuffle. How about this? I will see you for eight to ten visits and there will be no charge. I've been blessed in my own life in many ways and this will allow me to give something back to one of God's children."

Patty was overwhelmed by the doctor's proposal. "You are very kind to make the offer but that seems like such an imposition on your time. I would love to have you work with me but it really is too much."

"Not at all," replied the doctor. "When you are well and your life is back on track, just send me a note and let me know. That would be reward enough for me. Now let me look at my appointment book. How about next week at three p.m. on Monday? Is that okay for you?"

Patty was overwhelmed by Moke's generous offer and replied, "The time is fine and I will always be grateful to you." He gave her the appointment card and showed her out.

On the way home Patty kept thinking about the people and the events Dr. Moke asked about, people and events she had somehow been able to shut out of her thoughts as if they never existed and the events never occurred. As she drove, she said, "My ability to shut people out of my mind may well be one of my problems. I dealt with so many things simply by shutting them out. Denying they happened. And drugs helped me do it!" If Dr. Moke heard her comment, he would call it the beginning of insight.

Mary and Albert greeted Patty warmly when she got home. She told them about Dr. Moke including his willingness to see her for a limited time without charge. For the first time, she gave them some information about her background, that she was an only child and when she was eight her mother died of cancer. She told them a little about her difficult relationship with her father and that since she left San Francisco he knows nothing about her or where she is. Mary and Albert thanked Patty for trusting them enough to talk so freely.

Patty kept a regular schedule of Monday afternoon appointments with Dr. Moke. And he saw continuing progress on her part. Dr. Moke obtained the map of her life during the evaluation session. Now he needed to help her understand the map, the twists and turns of the road, the hazards and the responses of her fellow travelers and herself. He helped Patty travel the road once more but slowly and more as an outsider. She grew in her ability to understand the behavior of those on the road with her and in the light of that understanding to view her own behavior more carefully, more critically, and more lovingly....lovingly toward herself and "the others".... no longer from a distance. Dr. Moke was pleased with her progress and grateful that her insight developed so readily, as readily as he expected from his initial interview.

During their sixth session they were talking about Patty's relationship with her father and how she placed a barrier between them. Dr. Moke asked, "Have you ever thought of calling him? Don't answer that now. Just think about the question on your way back to Cave Junction today."

On the way home Patty realized she was feeling much differently about her father. Talking with Doctor Moke about Jim's behavior during her mother's illness and death brought a perspective totally new to her. She had never even considered what *he* was going through during those weeks and months. Now she found herself thinking of him as a person with complex, multiple burdens: one, her mother's death but also his loss of a loving wife, confidante and companion; two, a child needing attention, understanding and love; and three, his own feelings of inadequacy in caring for Patty. And there were also the demands of a busy law practice and the expectations of the senior partners and clients.

Moke suggested she might consider calling her father. She began to feel a longing to see him. She remembered walking with her hand in his when she was a little girl and playing rummy or catch with him even after her mother's illness began, but only for a few months and then it stopped. Even after her mother died he would usually come in her room and kiss her goodnight when he came home late from the office. She remembered how dazed he looked at times after her mother's death. She often saw him sitting in the living room gazing off into space. At times it seemed like he really wasn't there; and indeed he wasn't there for her some times, but that wasn't his fault. The death of her mother must have been so terribly hard for him. As she thought about them, it was obvious they loved each other dearly.

She thought about her quarrels with her father and how angry she used to get. Yes, she was a determined little girl and an even more determined teenager. Her father was so right about some of her behavior but their disagreements only pushed her into more defiance. Moke was right when he asked if she felt abandoned by her mother and as a result had unreal expectations for her father to cater to her needs. Then when Jim didn't see things the way Patty did, she saw it as another abandonment. It made her furious. Yes, she did overreact. And Doctor Moke had quietly asked if she might have done some abandoning in her own life.

As Patty drove into Cave Junction she decided to call her father. She considered asking Mary if she could call on the house phone. It wasn't to save the money for a pay phone. It was to know someone else who cared about her was in the room. With that thought she began to cry. *Someone there who cared about her!* How long had it been? Why did it happen? She thought of her father, of Kit, of Scott at McGregor's Jewelry, of Sister Dorothy in grade school, of Father Harvey in high school, of Grandmother Joan. None of them were there because *she abandoned them.* She said, "Damn it, Moke, you knew it all the time."

She waited until after seven, hoping her father would be home and wishing he might not be. She felt nervous about calling, wondering how he would respond. Would he be angry? Would he refuse to talk to her? She dialed. Someone picked up the phone.

Her father's voice: "Hello."

Patty: "Hi, Dad. It's Patty." She could hear him sobbing. It went on for some time.

Jim: "Patty, my love, my darling daughter. Where are you? How are you? I've missed you so terribly. I've thought about you every day, every night. I've prayed you'd come back or at least get in touch with me. You know your mother and I prayed to have you and God answered our prayer. I've been praying to find you or hear from you. You were a blessing in our lives and now it's a blessing to hear from you. Where are you? Can you come here or can I come there to see you? Do you need anything? Is everything okay? Are you well?"

Patty: "I'm okay, dad. I really am. I'm in Cave Junction, Oregon and currently living with a dear couple who have been and continue to be very kind to me. I've started seeing a psychiatrist who is most helpful."

Father and daughter continued their phone reunion for almost thirty minutes. Jim asked if they could get together. He was anxious to see her as soon as possible. When Patty thought about making this call, she decided if he wanted to see her it would be better to meet in a neutral place. If their first meeting was at home, it would begin with too many painful memories at least for her and probably for her father. She made the decision by choosing what she thought Moke would recommend. Patty said, "I would love to see you. Would you be able to come to Cave Junction this coming weekend? It's a long drive. Or you could check flights to the Medford airport and I could pick you up. The couple I live with run a motel. We'll have the best room available for you. Is it a possibility?"

Her father replied, "Let me have a quick look at my pocket calendar. Yes, this weekend would work well. As a matter of fact, I could come up on Friday and then return on Sunday. We have a good bit of catching up to do and that will give us time to at least begin it."

Patty said, "Wonderful, wonderful. I'll be looking forward to being with you by Friday evening. I love you, Dad. I'm glad you're coming. Oh, I'm at the Sleep Inn." Patty knew Jim was sobbing again as she heard him say, "I love you, Patty. See you Friday."

Mary and Albert were delighted with the news from Patty's call. Mary said she would give him the premier room which was a good bit nicer than the others. They invited Patty and her father to have Saturday dinner with them at the house. Mary was already planning the event. "Are there any foods your father doesn't like and does he have favorite foods?" she asked. Patty said she remembered very little about her father's likes or dislikes.

Jim arrived about seven-thirty Friday evening. He cried when he saw Patty and she joined him in tears as he embraced her, exclaiming, "My darling, darling daughter, I've missed you day and night since you've been gone. To see you again is a gift from God. I was almost giving up hope even though it's only been a matter of months."

Patty felt secure in his arms and his embrace blotted out any doubts she may have had. Mary and Albert came over when they heard the desk bell ring on Jim's entering. They were welcoming and expressed their gratitude for Patty' summer work and the pleasure they felt when she agreed to stay on with them for a while. Mary asked Patty to show Jim his room and bring him to the house to visit unless he was tired and wanted to retire.

Patty showed Jim his room and asked, "Is there anything you'd like to do after your long drive?"

Jim responded, "I'd just like to look at you and hear how things have been for you since I last saw you. Is there some place in town where we can get a soda and maybe some ice cream?"

Patty answered, "You sound like a kid, Dad, wanting ice cream. Sure, it's a couple of blocks from here. Let's walk." They walked and talked and had their ice cream and walked and talked returning to the motel. Then they talked some more. Patty could see Jim was looking tired from the long day and perhaps from all the talking. She went home a few minutes after nine.

The next day was cool and sunny and a day that beckoned them to see some sights as they talked some more. Patty fixed them a light breakfast at the house and then they went to see the Marble Halls of Oregon, more commonly called The Oregon Caves National Monument deep in the Siskiyou Mountains. The caves were formed as the rain water soaked through the ancient forest and over centuries morphed the limestone to marble. Patty suggested they take her car for the twenty-mile drive. Her father hadn't brought a jacket so she loaned him a wool cardigan which he willingly accepted when she told him the cave temperature year 'round was forty-four degrees.

Jim always had an interest in geology so the morning was a fascinating experience for him. It was also tiring. There are miles and miles of tunnels in the spreading caves. They took a park ranger guided tour which included going up five hundred steps, most of them high. The tour took over ninety minutes and was not recommended for anyone in poor health. Jim remarked, "I see the River Styx flows through the cave." Patty had never heard of the River Styx so he carefully explained the origin of the term. As he did so, Patty reflected on how helpful and warm and caring her father really is.

They left the caves and Patty drove to Gold Beach to the restaurant she ate at before. Then they spent a couple of hours walking on the beach. The time was full of talk about Jim's life, the relatives, Kit, and some about Jim's work which was going well. Patty talked frankly about her time in Haight-Ashbury, who she lived with, and her growing abuse of drugs. She said she ran away because she knew he was looking for her. Someone spotted the detective he hired. She spoke about her time in Cave Junction and how the kindness of Mary touched her deeply and helped her "cold turkey" with the drugs. She told him about therapy with Dr. Moke and how he mentioned calling her father.

It seemed they would never be able to quit talking, but Patty finally interrupted their conversation to say, "Dad, we better start for home. Mary and Albert are fixing a special dinner for the four of us to celebrate our reunion."

On the way home they were silent in the car, reflecting on all that was said. Jim finally broke the silence, "Patty, do you think you might consider coming home to live, at least for a time until you decide what you want to do with your life and where you might like to go? There would be no strings attached. You are your own person now and I respect that. In fact, I admire the progress you have made in dealing with the drug issue. I admire you for that and although hazards may remain I have confidence in you. You know how pleased Kit would be to have you back in the house even if only for a while."

Patty's first thought was, "I'd love to Dad" but she waited to reply. When she replied, "Let me think about it Dad. I'll see Dr. Moke again on Monday and I'd like to talk with him about it."

Jim replied, "Well, you know I'd love to have you a bit closer to home and of course living there or at least getting settled somewhere in the San Francisco area. It would be a gift to me and to Kit. She has continued to take some classes at the college and gives you credit for encouraging her studies." The two of them said no more that evening about Patty coming home.

They had a wonderful dinner and talked with Albert and Mary for over two hours. Patty kept thinking about dinner time at home when her mother stopped coming down long before she died, and then the uneasy dinners with Kit and her father which often became a question and answer period or a silent ritual. This evening was so different and so pleasant as they ate leisurely and talked and laughed. As the evening closed Mary mentioned they would be leaving at nine a.m. to go to their usual Sunday Mass in Gold Beach, so they said goodbye to Jim as he left for his room, Patty with him.

On the way Patty asked him when he would leave in the morning. Jim said he usually wakes early and expected to leave by seven or perhaps earlier if he woke earlier. He said he'd drive a while and then stop for breakfast in Crescent City where he planned to attend Sunday Mass. He continued, "I hope you will think seriously about my inviting you to come home, Patty. The place feels so empty and so lonely. Kit keeps busy with the house, her classes, lots of studying, and visits with her family. I don't see her very often. It will always be lonely until I can see you there again and even if you don't live with me to know you'll be back to see me occasionally. And whether you come back or not, please, let's always keep in touch."

Patty replied, "I am seriously thinking about it, Dad, and I will be in touch with you within the next week or two at the most. By then I'll decide; I promise. And thanks for coming, Dad. I have enjoyed this time with you. It's made me think about a lot of things including my own poor behavior and my unhealthy defensiveness about it. I wasn't easy for you to deal with at times. I'm sorry. Perhaps I'm beginning to grow up; I hope."

Jim responded, "I had a hard time when your mother died and also during her illness. I'm afraid I often focused on Susan and then on my woes when she died. And I saved little time for my daughter. I need some forgiveness from you for many things. Talk and time will help us mend the past. Goodbye, my dear Patty. I will pray to see you soon." They were both teary-eyed as they said goodnight and goodbye.

Sunday was a thought-filled day for Patty. She covered the motel office until Mary and Albert returned. Then she drove to Gold Beach for lunch and spent the afternoon by the ocean. She kept thinking about her appointment on Monday and wondering what Dr. Moke would say about the visit.

On Monday Patty arrived ten minutes early for her appointment. Dr. Moke opened his office door when she entered the waiting room. She was glad he invited her in even though it was early. After they sat down, Moke nodded to her as he usually did, meaning she should start. Patty was ready. "Guess what! My father visited me this weekend. I called him last Monday as you suggested and he was anxious to see me. It was a great visit. We got along wonderfully. We talked for hours. He asked me to come back home at least for a while until I decide what I want to do. I told him about you and he was glad I was seeing someone. I told him I wanted to talk to you before I decided about going home. I've been thinking about it all and I was anxious to see you today." Patty stopped for breath. "And that's my story today."

Doctor Moke smiled and quietly said, "I don't remember suggesting you call your father. I think I asked you if *you ever thought* about calling him. I asked you not to answer my question but suggested you might think about my question on the way home. Apparently you thought about it and made *your* decision. Congratulations on what was apparently an important life decision. You now have that ability, Patty. Let me emphasize that for you. *You are now able to think wisely and clearly.* You no longer respond mentally, emotionally or physically to your prior need for drugs. Think about that for a while, Patty. Consider what a treasure that is: to think with clarity, to consider possibilities, to make decisions about your life now and about your future. And to do that carefully and calmly, considering the pros and cons of the situation. It doesn't mean you won't make mistakes. We all make mistakes. But to make a mistake because drugs have poisoned your thinking or because a desire for drugs blotted out everything else, that's not a mistake, that's a tragedy.

"Now you're here and I hope that look on your face means you're happy and pleased with what happened because of *your* decision a week ago. So now I'm anxious to hear more from that competent mind of yours. I'm sure you spent most of the morning considering your immediate future."

Dr. Moke's words strengthened Patty's self-assurance and supported her thought process. During her morning drive she tentatively decided she would go to live with her father at least for a time. But she wanted Dr. Moke to support her decision. After his comments, she realized she didn't need his approval. She could decide! Patty spoke, "I think it is time for me to go home. It will be helpful for me to have the support of my father and of Kit. My father told me I will have my independence, but I'm not sure I'm ready to be completely on my own. I can well benefit from his presence and at times his advice. And Kit is a young woman with her own store of female wisdom. Actually it seems almost miraculous that I feel as good as I do and as positive about my life. I know all is not perfect in my world or anyone else's but I'm in a much better state of mind to meet the challenges of living. I need to tell you how you've brought a peace to my mind and my soul that I never expected to find again."

Dr. Moke said, "Thank you for your kind words. Our time is about up. Did you want to make our usual appointment for next Monday?"

Patty looked at him and saw again that faint smile she had sometimes seen before. She said, "I guess I wasn't thinking about coming next week. Do you think I should have another appointment?"

Moke's smile broadened as he replied, "I'm available, but I think you should decide the question about another appointment."

It was Patty's turn to smile as she answered, "It would be a long drive from San Francisco so we might have to make it later in the day." Dr. Moke laughed. The matter was obviously settled. Patty continued, "I can never thank you enough for your care, Doctor Moke. You were a God-send in my life. I will always remember your words and the powerful influence they had on my thinking. I can never repay you for the change you brought to my life. You generously saw me without charging a fee. When I'm working again I want to send you the money I would have paid for your care."

Dr. Moke responded, "No, no. Please, don't. To observe the changes you have made in your thinking and to know that you are on a healthy course for the future and that you are reconciled with your family, all of that is payment for me. Let me do this in gratitude to God for blessings in my own life. There is one thing you can do for me. Later on when things are settled for you and life is stable and healthy and good, I would appreciate it if you would just send me a card with the words: All is well."

As she stood to leave, she offered her hand to Dr. Moke. He held it with both of his saying, "Goodbye and God bless you, Patty."

It was nine months later when an insured package came to Dr. Stephen Moke with a return address: McGregor Jewelry, San Francisco. Dr. Moke opened the package. The note read: "All is well. I fashioned this for your wife. Patty (the girl who wandered)." Enclosed was a necklace with a simple metal band that held a greenish gem stone with light shades of gold and encircled by a gold band. A jeweler friend told him it was a valuable chrysoprase gem stone thought to promote joy and happiness and healing of the heart energies of depression and anxiety. Whenever Ann, Doctor Moke's wife, wore the necklace, they always remembered Patty.

THE WOMAN WHO WAS SILENT

Susan Hanson was arrested for murder in March of the year 1966. There was something unusual about Susan after her arrest. She refused to say a word to anyone. She would not talk to the police or detectives or personnel in the jail. After the first forty-eight hours in the Seattle Municipal jail she was taken before a judge, the Honorable Thomas Charles, to determine her charge and appropriate place of incarceration. She was mute and could not be persuaded to speak. She was returned to her cell.

Judge Charles had a psychiatrist friend who was the Superintendent of the Braceland Psychiatric Institute, in Tacoma. When he returned to his chambers he called Stephen Moke, M.D. When they were connected Charles began, "Hello, Steve. This is Tom, Tom Charles. I haven't seen you in a while. I'm calling to ask a favor if you can oblige. I saw a very unusual defendant in my court today. The police report states she murdered a neighbor woman, someone with whom she had apparently been friends for a long time. In fact, the murder weapon, a knife, was still in her hand when the police arrived. She was arrested and placed in jail the day before yesterday. Today they brought her to my court for arraignment. The officer stated the basic facts and said she had refused to talk to anyone since her arrest. She would not respond to anything I said to her and never even looked at me. She'd look at the ceiling, the floor or just stare ahead as if nothing was there. Is there any possibility you could drive up here in the next couple of days and see her? I would feel more comfortable if I had the benefit of your expertise."

Doctor Moke replied, "It's good to hear your voice, Tom. Let me look at my schedule while I ask how Margaret and the children are. Ah, here we are. I could be there the day after tomorrow. Suppose I see her at ten a.m. and perhaps we could have lunch together at noon and I'll give you my opinion, providing she will even talk to me."

Tom answered, "Margaret and the children are fine. Thanks for asking. Thursday will be great. I'll arrange lunch at the Seattle Club. Will look forward to catching up a bit in addition to whatever you can tell me about Susan Hanson, the woman you will be seeing and hopefully talking with. I will call Warden Hover and make arrangements for you to see her."

Doctor Moke left at nine a.m. Thursday morning, allowing plenty of time for the thirty-five mile trip to Seattle. He stopped at a doughnut shop near the jail, had some coffee and looked at the morning paper until it was close to interview time. He got a small notebook from his car and walked two blocks to the jail. On entering he went through the search and questions. Then a guard took him to Susan Hanson's cell. It was a cell about ten feet square with three solid walls and the entry door in a wall of iron bars so the occupant was visible at all times. On the wall opposite the door there was a wooden bench about five feet long. There was a bed on one side of the room and a toilet and sink on the other. Susan was sitting on the end of the bench staring at the bed. Moke estimated her to be about forty to forty-five years old, medium height and build, brown hair, hands motionless in her lap. The guard asked Moke if he wanted to enter the cell. He replied in the affirmative; so the guard unlocked and opened the door, let him in and locked the door behind him saying, "Just call when you want to leave."

As he approached Susan Hanson he introduced himself. "Ms. Hanson, I'm Doctor Stephen Moke. Judge Thomas Charles, whom you saw in court two days ago, has asked me to come and see you. He told me you did not respond to any of his questions in the courtroom and that you have not spoken to anyone here at the jail. The record indicates you were arrested last Sunday, five days ago. Do you mind if I sit here?" He approached and pointed to the other end of the bench. Ms. Hanson neither looked up nor responded. He sat down.

Doctor Moke spoke slowly and softly without any note of threat or demand in his voice. There was a definite gentleness in his tone and manner. "I hope you will at least consider talking to me. . . I know that something happened last Sunday and after it happened the police came and brought you here to the city jail. . . Could you tell me a little about what happened on Sunday?"

Doctor Moke left a space of several seconds between each sentence. He gave the impression time was not pressing and he would be patient. After the above statements he sat quietly and calmly on the bench for three or four minutes. When he first sat down, Susan Hanson dropped her gaze to her hands and now continued looking at them.

Moke continued, "There is some reason you are here in the jail. . . . Could you talk to me about it? . . . Can you tell me something about what happened last Sunday? . . . I'm sure you must have some memories of what occurred. . . . If you talk to me, I *may* be able to help you. . . . Whatever you tell me I will report to Judge Thomas. . . . He is a friend of mine and I know he is a good man. . . . He too will try to help you." A pause between each sentence and each word spoken slowly, softly, almost soothingly.

Doctor Moke continued comments similar to and repetitive of those above. This went on for over twenty minutes. On his way to the jail he decided this might or might not be a success or even a total failure. He realized it was important not to show any frustration or irritation even if nothing positive came of the visit. He finally decided Ms. Hanson was not going to speak to him. He said with the same calm and softness, again leaving a few seconds between sentences, "I will have to be leaving soon . . . and I don't think the judge will allow me to see you again. . . I'm sorry you feel you are not ready to talk to me . . . because I believe you would feel better. . . if you talked. . . at least a little. . . No one is going to punish you for not talking . . . but it does make it difficult for persons at the jail . . . and for the judge to know . . . what might be best for you. . . I'll say goodbye now . . . and when the guard opens the door. . . I will be on my way. . . I do hope you will find someone . . . with whom you will be able to talk."

Doctor Moke stood up, took the few steps to the door and called, "Guard." The guard came and as he unlocked the door, Susan Hanson made a throated sound. It was not a word. It was like the sound one makes in clearing one's throat. Moke turned to look at her. She had raised her head and was looking at him. He asked the guard to leave and he went back and sat beside her.

Painfully, slowly, haltingly Susan Hanson told Doctor Moke why she stabbed her neighbor with a butcher knife last Sunday morning. And then, in the same slow manner, she told him about the lengthy relationship she and her husband had with the victim and her husband. She went on to tell him about the Saturday evening before the happening (as she called it). She told him what made her decide to kill Lucille Blair. Doctor Moke chose not to probe too deeply at this time but asked a few questions which enabled him to determine Susan Hanson's state of mind at the time of the "happening." He also assessed her current mental and emotional condition in order to make suitable recommendations to Judge Thomas.

They talked about thirty minutes; some of it spontaneous but most of it in response to Moke's questions and patiently waiting for answers. Finally, Doctor Moke told Susan he would see Judge Thomas later that day and he would pass on to the Judge the information she had given him. He added that at this time he could not discuss with her any recommendation he might have for the judge. He stood to go and said, "Thank you, Ms. Hanson, for talking to me. Judge Thomas and personnel at the desk told me your husband, Oscar, has been eager to visit you. I will mention it to Judge Thomas and I feel certain he will make arrangements for your husband to visit. Goodbye, thank you again and I hope things go well for you."

To Moke's total surprise Ms. Hanson extended her hand and said, "Thank you. I appreciate your coming."

After Doctor Moke left the jail he walked to a nearby park and sat on a bench to write notes in his book. He took no notes during their conversation out of concern that note-taking might add a more formal and threatening atmosphere and as a result make Ms. Hanson more reluctant to speak freely. He also realized there may well come a time when he would be talking about this interview in court and even though it revealed some startling things he was not likely to ever forget, written notes would make him a more convincing and accurate witness. After he finished writing he left the notes in his car and walked the six blocks to the Seattle Club to meet Judge Charles.

Thomas was seated waiting in the entrance lounge. They greeted each other with a handshake and various comments as they were escorted to their table. During lunch they chatted about family news and some of their friends from college days at Gonzaga University in Spokane where they were both undergraduates. As they sat with coffee at the end of the meal, Stephen gave Thomas his report about Susan Hanson. He described Ms. Hanson's behavior with some detail and then reported their conversation. In final comment he said, "At this point, Tom, I think Ms. Hanson should be sent to the Braceland Psychiatric Institute for continuing evaluation and treatment as needed until she is able to stand trial for the murder of

Lucille Blair. Whether or not the State's Attorney's Office will agree to that depends on you."

"Well, that's quite a story and you have certainly given me the pieces I need to proceed as you suggest," Judge Charles replied. "I'll discuss it with the State's Attorney and if she insists on a court procedure I may have to call you to testify. She's usually good to deal with and I think the information you've given me is persuasive enough. If possible I'd rather not subject Ms. Hanson to another court appearance. I believe it can be settled in camera. And now I see by my watch I should be heading back to court. I'm due back on the bench in twenty minutes."

Steve commented, "You probably need some extra time to get your wig on straight."

Tom chuckled and said, "One would help cover my bald spot you know. Maybe that's why those old timers used them. I want to thank you again for your willingness to come up today, Steve. I was uneasy about this situation and felt uncomfortable keeping Ms. Hanson in jail with the possibility of dragging her back and forth to the court every few days. My impression was she just might well have maintained her silence forever. I thought I could depend on your psychiatric skills. I'm familiar with them from testimony you've given in my court. Have a safe trip home and give our regards to Ann. The four of us should get together before we get too old to travel."

As they shook hands, Steve said, "It's been good to see you, Tom. I think we'll both be traveling for another forty or fifty years. Nonetheless let's have dinner together soon. Thanks for the opportunity to get involved in a fascinating case. By the way, if the State's Attorney wants to ask me any questions, tell her to give me a call. Thanks again."

Judge Charles walked away briskly and Doctor Moke strolled leisurely to his car, reflecting on their luncheon conversation; and as he drove home recalling old friends and good times during their Gonzaga years.

On Monday of the following week the Braceland Psychiatric Institute was notified the sheriff from King's County would be bringing a Ms. Susan Hanson to the hospital Wednesday afternoon. The court stipulated she was to be housed on a secure unit at all times. Available records would accompany the patient.

When Doctor Moke heard the news he called the front desk and asked where Frank Blair was working that afternoon. Frank, the husband of the woman whom Susan Hanson murdered, was a member of the hospital building and grounds crew. Doctor Moke had seen Frank the previous week to offer condolences. When he learned where Frank was, Moke walked over to see him and told him Ms. Hanson would be a patient at the hospital, was coming on Wednesday and would be there for an unknown period of time. He added, "Ms. Hanson will be cared for in Building #3. I will ask your supervisor not to send you to work in that building. If anyone should happen to ask you to do anything in that building, tell them you have been ordered not to enter Building #3 and if they need a reason tell them to call my office."

The day Susan Hanson was admitted to the hospital Doctor Moke went to see her briefly. He told her he was the one who recommended to Judge Thomas that she be brought to this facility for care and supervision until she was considered competent to stand trial for the murder of Lucille Blair. He explained to her, as he was Superintendent of the Hospital, he would not personally be her treating psychiatrist. He would assign Doctor Ralph Rogers as her psychiatrist. He would keep in touch with Doctor Rogers regarding her progress and he would come by occasionally to see how things were going for her.

Doctor Moke decided not to tell Doctor Rogers about the contents of his conversation with Ms. Hanson during the jail interview. First of all, there was a doctor-patient relationship which he could probably waive under the circumstances. Secondly, he could ask the patient for permission to discuss the contents of their jail meeting with Doctor Rogers. He chose to ignore both possibilities on the grounds that Doctor Rogers needed to develop a therapeutic relationship with Ms. Rogers sufficient to bring all that information into their treatment sessions. If Ms. Hanson wanted Doctor Rogers to know the information it was either up to her to tell him or up to him to discover the trail that would lead him there. Doctor Moke asked Doctor Rogers to keep in touch with him about Ms. Hanson every two or three weeks.

It was ten months later during Doctor Rogers' regular report to Doctor Moke when the two of them discussed Ms. Hanson's readiness to stand trial. Doctor Rogers said he thought Ms. Hanson was of sufficient capacity to understand the nature of trial proceedings and the ability to cooperate with her attorneys. He felt certain she would pass the question of *mens re*. Doctor Moke agreed based on his own occasional visits and review of the ongoing record. He told Doctor Rogers he would inform Judge Charles of their agreement.

Later that afternoon Moke called Judge Charles and told him their current position regarding Ms. Hanson. As they discussed the matter, the Judge asked, "Once the trial date is set, do you think Ms. Hanson should remain in the hospital until a day or two before the day of trial?"

Doctor Moke completely agreed saying, "Undoubtedly that would be the best course. Her attorneys can visit her here until the time of trial. By interviewing her here, they will more likely get her full cooperation. She is comfortable with the hospital staff and her surroundings. Interviewing her in jail would be, to say the least, unsettling for her. Do you know if her husband has engaged an attorney?"

Judge Thomas responded, "I believe he has but I'm not sure. I suggest you call her husband and check. I'm sure you have his phone number."

Doctor Moke replied, "We do. In fact, Mr. Hanson stopped by my office a couple of times to ask about Susan. He visits her often and seems to be attentive to her. I'll call him and tell him about our recommendation and that we're getting close to trial. When you set the trial date, let me know and we'll plan to bring Susan to the jail two days before the trial.

"By the way, when Susan came here we had instructions to keep her on a secure unit at all times. I would like to change it to 'grounds privileges' as ordered by Doctor Rogers, her treating psychiatrist. Can you verbally authorize me to do that?" Thomas asked what was meant by "grounds privileges." After Moke told him it meant "freedom to walk on the Institute grounds when accompanied by a staff member," Judge Thomas said it was fine with him and there was no need for written approval. It was a hospital prerogative.

Moke called the front desk and asked if Oscar Hanson was currently visiting his wife. The desk clerk said he signed in fifteen minutes ago and he usually stays about thirty minutes. Moke told the clerk, "When Mr. Hanson comes to sign out, please ask him if he has time to stop by the Superintendent's office."

About twenty minutes later the front desk clerk called and said, "Mr. Hanson is on the way over." Moke's secretary soon buzzed him to tell him Mr. Hanson was there.

Moke went to the waiting room to greet him. "Mr. Hanson, come on in. Thanks for coming by. I asked you to come because there are new developments as of thirty minutes ago. I just talked with Judge Thomas, the man who sent your wife here for care. I told him Doctor Rogers and I both consider Susan competent to stand trial. The plan will go like this: Susan will remain here until two days before the trial date (which is still to be set) and then she will be transferred to the Seattle Municipal Jail. I wanted to ask you if you have an attorney. I presume you do but I'm not aware of any attorneys visiting her. Since she's in a psychiatric hospital I presume they may be getting most of their information from other sources, perhaps assuming hospitalization here automatically conveys a taint of unreliability. They will surely want to acquaint themselves with her in person and discuss their preparations for trial.

Mr. Hanson replied, "Yes, I've hired the law firm of Craven and Crotty for our defense. They seem to be very busy. Robert Craven will be the lead attorney and it's difficult to get in touch with him. He tells me he recently finished a complex and lengthy case. I'll ask him to get in touch with you sometime when he's here to visit Susan. By the way, I'm sure you know the husband of the deceased works on the grounds crew here. Frank is a good man and has shown no evidence of being vindictive. We run into each other quite often. He lives across the street from me. We speak and occasionally stop to talk."

Doctor Moke said, "Yes, when Susan came here I got in touch with Frank and told him Susan was coming. His supervisor tells me he's a good worker and seems to be a kind person. By the way, he has been asked not to do any work in Building #3 where Susan is housed; and we will arrange things so if Susan is out on the grounds there will be no possibility of her running into Frank. I should tell you we now have permission for Susan to walk on the grounds with an attendant. I got approval from the judge the last time we talked.

"Thanks for coming over. If there're any questions or any problems, please give me a call or stop by." As he was leaving Oscar commented about how well the hospital treats him and how he appreciates the care Susan is getting.

Two days later Doctor Moke had a call from Robert Craven asking if they could get together. They agreed to meet the following Monday over lunch at the hospital as suggested by Moke. The receptionist was prepared for the visit and someone escorted the attorney to Moke's office. Doctor Moke had arranged to have lunch in the private dining room adjacent to his office.

As they were eating Mr. Craven talked about the Hanson trial with an air of confidence bordering on entitlement. His attitude suggested there could be no question about his requests which to Moke sounded more like demands. He wanted the freedom to talk privately with Susan Hanson at any time. He wanted to review her complete record from the day of admission until the time of her trial and to copy any part of her record for his case-file.

When Mr. Craven finished his requests Doctor Moke looked pensive and delayed answering immediately. He chose his words carefully. "You may visit Ms. Hanson during visiting hours and the charge nurse will arrange a private room for your visits. The visiting hours are two to four p.m. and seven to nine p.m. seven days a week. You might consider arranging your visits with Mrs. Hanson's husband so you will not be in conflict with his visiting schedule. That is up to you. But if he is visiting his wife when you come, his visit takes precedence.

"About the medical records, those you may not look at or copy in any way. Government regulations insist we maintain the privacy of all medical records without the written permission of the patient or of a person who has power of attorney for the patient. You can draw up a request for release of records and request Ms. Hanson sign the release. In which case, Doctor Rogers, her treating psychiatrist, will advise her not to sign the release of records because it will be seen by Ms. Hanson as potentially threatening. From a treatment point of view, and that's what we are about here, any release of records could be detrimental to the emotional well-being of the patient. Now, you can take all this to the trial judge for a decision if you choose. It might buy you time, because a hearing would delay the trial, but it will *not* get you the medical records."

After a short delay Mr. Craven responded, "I think you're being rather tight-fisted about the visits and the records but I'm not going to waste time going to court or trying to change your mind. Thanks for the lunch. I guess we'll see you in court." He left abruptly.

Moke realized that while he could control Susan's hospital records he needed access to reliable details of her past life in order to prepare for his later testimony. Her life history was a major part of her medical record but was sparse on details. He thought it would be wise to have a source other than Susan to verify and if need be to expand on those details. He decided to call Oscar Hanson and enlist his cooperation. When he made the contact, Oscar said he would be happy to discuss Susan's and his own past history and meet with Moke any time.

The details of Susan's life became of utmost importance since it was obvious the question of mental capacity would be the crux of the trial. Her attorneys would search though all available documents and more importantly contact everyone they could find who knew her. Susan began meeting with her attorney, Robert Craven, every Monday during the evening visiting hours. Craven decided he needed corroboration of much of what she said. He appealed to various staff members to gain information about her care and treatment but they referred him to Doctor Rogers or the Superintendent. Rogers' responses were severely limited and Craven never approached Doctor Moke.

These are the details of Susan Hanson's life as shown on her hospital record and as expanded by her husband. Susan was born in Seattle, Washington on July 3rd, 1922, the seven pound, six-ounce daughter of Olaf and Florence Larson. She was a healthy baby and developed normally through her early years. Her mother was a stay at home mom who delighted in the care of their only child. Other than whooping cough at age three and measles at age twelve there was no history of significant illness.

Susan's father, Olaf, was an intelligent hard working man, respected by his peers. His parents were immigrants from Norway and came to Seattle in the late eighteen hundreds. Olaf had completed high school but lacking financial wherewithal decided to go into manual trades. Olaf Larson worked as a carpenter for several years and then signed on for an apprenticeship at Call Clark Electric Company, a union shop. He completed his apprenticeship and worked there as a journeyman for three years. The Clark Company also had a plumbing shop. Olaf transferred to the plumbing shop and completed a two-year apprenticeship. Before long he was working for Seattle Gas and Electric where he had a successful career and eventually became Director of the Company.

Olaf and his wife, Florence, were practicing Catholics and attended Sunday Mass at St. Edward's Church in downtown Seattle. Susan, their only child, attended Saint Edward's Catholic School from kindergarten through high school and later went to Seattle University, a Jesuit college.

It was noted in Susan's hospital record that when she was about ten years old she began bringing home poor grades. She was normally one of the top students in her class. A midyear report was C's and even a couple of D's. Doctor Rogers explored the issue; his recorded notes indicated Susan was sleeping poorly during that time and "felt uneasy and frightened." On questioning by Doctor Rogers Susan couldn't identify any reason, saying "Everything was fine at home" according to Doctor Rogers notes. There were no problems with peers or teachers. Susan had no explanation. She thought it lasted three months or more; then all was fine again. When

Doctor Moke read that entry, he made a note in the little booklet he carried, "Ask about the poor grade period when she was ten."

He went back to "family history" in the record and later expanded some of it through talks with Oscar Hanson. During her junior year of college as a liberal arts student, she met Oscar Hanson at a social function for young parishioners. Oscar was four years older than Susan and was at the time a foreman at the Lockheed Ship Building and Construction Company. They were immediately attracted to each other and began dating. The couple met both sets of parents and in their visiting discovered all their grandparents emigrated from Norway and eventually came to the Seattle area. Susan's grandfather worked in the building trades and Oscar's in the shipping industry. Susan and Oscar were engaged to be married during Susan's third year of college. They married the year after Susan graduation. Susan's father died six years later at the age of seventy-six from a cerebral hemorrhage. Susan's mother died of breast cancer at age seventy-four, two years after the father's death.

The patient's history also noted that Susan's father ran for mayor of Seattle when Susan was age 18. An accompanying note by Doctor Rogers, "As Susan was finishing high school there was a marked change in her behavior. She had been popular with classmates and enthusiastically involved in activities. She was on the girls' volley ball team. She was co-chair of the senior dance committee. Less than three months before graduation Susan quit the volley ball team, resigned from the dance committee and spent minimal time with classmates at the school or after school." Moke made a note in his little book: "what happened at high school graduation time."

Now that he was delving into this history, Doctor Moke needed some fill-in information about Oscar Hanson. During one of Oscar's visits he asked Oscar to tell him something about himself. Oscar said, "I'm the youngest of three boys, all living in Washington. My oldest brother works for the Federal Forest Service and the middle brother teaches at Seattle Pacific University. Both are married and have children."

Doctor Moke asked if he and his wife planned to have children when they married. As he asked the question he added, "I know that's a personal question but it might fit in somewhere as I interview Susan prior to her trial."

Oscar replied, "I understand and the question is fine. Yes, we did plan on having children when we married. As you probably know, our religion was rigidly opposed to birth control at that time. I believe they've softened their stance a bit on the subject. We were not using birth control but Susan did not get pregnant. We were married five years when quite unintentionally I discovered she was avoiding intercourse during likely times of fertility. I happened to look at a calendar she kept in her night stand. She accidentally left it out one day. She was distraught when I discovered it but she did not deny the truth of her birth-control plan. For three months she refused to talk about *why*. But she insisted we could not have sex unless we continued the calendar method or used contraception. It was not a problem for me to use a condom but it was difficult to give up the possibility of having a child. After a lapse of time she began talking about her fear of an evil in our country, an evil which would destroy our way of life. I remember her words, 'the devil will soon rule.' I couldn't believe she was talking that way. It was so unlike her. She refused to say anything further about it and over the months and years it became a thing of the past."

Doctor Moke made a mental note to check with Susan regarding "reason for birth control." Then he replied, "I appreciate your candor in regard to such a private subject. Were there any other incidents you might recall when Susan behaved or talked in a rather unusual or surprising manner?"

Oscar was silent for a minute or more after Moke's question. Then he responded, "About ten years ago we often visited a couple, Edith and Joe Tracey, whom we knew from our parish. The four of us were talking about the newspapers we customarily read and the shows and news we listened to on the radio and watched on TV. They mentioned a prominent clergyman who had been giving regular talks on the radio, weekly I think. Fulton Sheen was his name. We told the Traceys we never heard of him. The Traceys said Sheen was now on television. They raved about him as a dynamic speaker and said his show titled *Life Is Worth Living* was both moving and enlightening. He would be speaking the following Sunday and they invited us to dinner to hear and see Sheen in action. After the presentation we unanimously agreed it was a marvelous talk and he was a remarkable speaker.

"We continued watching Sheen's Sunday shows for weeks. Then Susan suddenly refused to watch any more. She never told me why and I didn't press the matter because I was never as enthusiastic about Sheen as other people seemed to be. A couple of months after that, the Traceys were invited to our house for Sunday dinner. After dinner Edith Tracey suggested we watch Sheen's lecture. I turned the television to the channel when the show began. Susan said she wasn't feeling well and left the room as the three of us continued to watch Sheen. I still have no idea what happened that evening. After the Traceys left, Susan came out of the bedroom and we cleaned up from dinner. When I asked how she was, she said she felt fine. Strangely enough after that night she always made excuses when I said anything about visiting the Traceys. I never knew why. We never visited with them again."

Moke made another mental note: "talk with Susan about stopping visits to the Traceys." "I'm grateful for your ability to remember incidents like this, Oscar, so if you remember other occasions when Susan behaved in an unexpected way, a way you couldn't understand at the time, let me know. Incidents like you just told me may be of value when we get to Susan's trial.

"Now would you tell me a little about you and your wife's relationship with the Blair's? Had you known them for some time? Were they good friends or just casual neighbors? Did the two of you spend much time with the two of them?"

Oscar answered, "They've been our neighbors for about eight years. I would say we were very good friends for the last five. We saw them quite regularly and probably every month had dinner together at their house or ours. On occasion we went out to dinner with them 'Dutch treat.' In fact, we were out to dinner the night before the tragedy. We usually go to the small dining room at Harrah's Casino. It was a pleasant evening, but I remember when we were back in our house Susan said, 'When Lucille got up to go to the bathroom I wonder why she stopped to talk to those strangers at a table near the restroom door.' In fact, Susan repeated the comment when we got in bed. The whole thing seemed insignificant to me. I never noticed it and all the people in the restaurant (there weren't more than thirty) were probably strangers to me." Mock made a mental note "have Craven put husband on stand and ask about evening before the murder."

Oscar continued, "I would say Lucille was probably Susan's best friend, perhaps her only friend. They often shopped together and exchanged recipes and talked about clothes and make-up and things like that. We knew a number of people from the Catholic community at our church but we seldom went to any of their social activities. Susan didn't make friends easily. I always felt she was somewhat wary of people."

Susan's hospital record showed that soon after she graduated from college she began working at the local Social Security Office. She was in the accounting department. The record indicated she left the job abruptly two years ago. There was nothing in the record about the circumstances of her leaving. Moke asked Oscar why Susan retired from her job at Social Security just one year before she would have been eligible for retirement benefits. Oscar thought for a while before answering. "That's a few years ago now, give me a moment. I remember I was surprised by her decision. It came very abruptly. She came home from work one day and just said, 'I retired today.' When I asked 'what happened,' Susan simply said, 'I can't work for people I can't trust.' She wouldn't say anything more when I asked her whom she couldn't trust and what they were doing that was untrustworthy. That's how Susan was about people. She could harbor doubts so readily. And rarely would she explain her reasoning." Doctor Moke made another mental note: "reason for retiring from social security."

Oscar and Moke talked for almost an hour. Moke ended their conversation saying, "This was extremely helpful, Oscar. The information you gave me today will be of value in preparing my testimony for Susan's trial. I should be hearing from Judge Charles any day now. He will set a trial date depending on his own calendar and the availability of the State Prosecutor and your attorney, Mr. Craven. I believe our talk today will have a significant effect on the outcome of the trial so it was time well spent."

Oscar commented as he left, "Thanks for your time and your interest. I pray for a favorable outcome. Susan is one of the gentlest people I have ever known. It's still hard for me to believe she could have done what she did. I lay awake at night thinking about it and thinking she couldn't have done it. It makes no sense to me. I just can't understand it all. I have to force myself to accept the reality of it. But now that we've talked so much about Susan, it reminds me she did have times when she seemed extremely preoccupied and withdrawn, with not much to say and unwilling to discuss things. She would appear worried and look like she was inwardly struggling with something. I sort of got used to it and decided it was just part of her world. What we've said today brings it back for me to wonder about."

Oscar and Moke ended their talk agreeing they would keep in touch and if Oscar remembered any other unusual incidents he'd give Doctor Moke a call.

After Oscar left, Doctor Moke sat wondering how he could best approach these questions with Susan. He felt certain he had her complete confidence. He needed to be sure he didn't lose it. He had to lead her carefully and slowly and gently to be open about questions he would raise.

Their relationship was based on her initial willingness to confide during his visit to the jail. On that occasion Susan revealed secrets she had never revealed to anyone. In the hospital record it was noted she claimed she could not remember anything she did that fateful morning until she realized she was standing by her friend's body, holding a bloody knife in her hand.

Doctor Moke was aware there was a different bond between Susan and himself. He was confident it was still there but he knew it had to be carefully preserved. Since her admission to the hospital he had visited her intermittently, often enough to maintain the connection they had. He was careful not to overshadow her relationship with Doctor Rogers who remained her primary therapist since the day of her admission. Moke and Rogers maintained professional clarity and boundaries in their relationship with Susan and with each other. They agreed from the beginning that Rogers would be her therapist and Moke would be the "investigating psychiatrist" and primary witness at Susan's trial. His initial interview with Susan was the *key* to her defense. Doctor Moke was looking to discover additional information from Susan's life to support the validity of her responses that day in the jail. He had not revealed the content of his jail interview with Susan to anyone except Judge Charles.

Doctor Moke talked to Doctor Rogers about the several areas he wanted to explore further with Susan. Rogers commented, "None of the questions you mentioned came up in my conversations with Susan. Some of the events are noted in Susan's record but I presume were passed over as non-significant. Oscar's comments may introduce a new dimension of Susan's life. It's fortunate you have Oscar's trust and took the time to uncover more detail. I hope your conversations with Susan and Oscar help build a case for acquittal. I can't imagine how permanently damaging it would be for Susan if she were sent to prison."

Doctor Moke spent some time thinking over his hypothesis regarding Susan's motivation for killing Lucille Blair. He decided it might be worthwhile to ask Frank Blair about the evening he and his wife spent with the Hanson's the night before the murder. He called the Building and Grounds Supervisor's office and asked it Frank Blair was at work that day. He was; so Doctor Moke asked the supervisor to send Blair to his office. Moke added, "He's not in any trouble so don't think that's why I'm calling. It's just a personal matter."

Blair arrived a few minutes later. Doctor Moke asked him to come into the office and explained, "Thanks for coming over, Frank. I wanted to ask you something about the evening you and your wife spent with the Hanson's the night before your wife's tragic death. As you recall the evening, can you remember anything unusual about it, anything that was said, actions of anyone on the way or coming home? Knowing your address, I assume you drove to the restaurant. Did you go in one car or did you go separately?"

Blair replied, "We went together in my car. We always went together and took turns on cars. I drove that night. About that evening, nothing unusual comes to mind. Well, one thing was a little unusual but not of any significance. Lucille always sat with me when I drove. That's how it usually turned out. Lucille and I front or back and Oscar and Susan sitting together. As we got in the car to go home, Susan said, 'Let Lucille sit in the back with me so I can keep an eye on her.' She laughed a little and we all laughed, but I remember now, it crossed my mind that she seemed serious when she said it and then kind of laughed to cover it up."

Moke said, "Nothing else special that evening?"

Blair answered, "Now that you bring the evening to my mind, Susan seemed a little quiet when Lucille came back to the table after going to the ladies' room. I just thought she may have felt Lucille should have asked her if she wanted to go too. All in all, I'd say it was just the usual night with our two best friends."

Doctor Moke said, "Well, thanks for stopping by Frank. I told your supervisor it was a personal matter and had nothing to do with your work at the hospital. I understand you are a valued employee. Thanks for that too." They shook hands and Frank left. And Moke made another mental note: "check on talk to stranger" and "ride home in back seat."

The following morning Doctor Moke decided it was time he approached Susan Hanson to begin his preparation for her trial. When they were together in her room with "Privacy" card on the door, he began, "Susan, you know that Judge Charles, the judge who sent you here, will be setting a date for your trial for the murder of Lucille Blair. I'm sure you recall the conversation we had when you were in jail. I've never discussed that conversation with anyone except Judge Charles as I told you I would do. Now I will need your permission to report on that conversation when I testify at your trial. Do I have your permission to reveal, during your trial, the content of our conversation in the jail?" Susan nodded and spoke her assent. Dr. Moke continued. "You are in a far better state of mind today than you were that first day I met you. Now you understand the significance of what you told me and you are able to cooperate with your attorney and those preparing you for trial. First, I want to ask you, have you told your attorney the things you told me that morning in the jail?"

Susan seemed hesitant as she replied, "It was difficult but I did tell him about my fear of Lucille and generally why I was afraid of her, but I find it difficult to be open with him about the details. He's okay but I can't trust him like I trust you and Doctor Rogers and the staff here. Of course, I haven't told everything to Doctor Rogers or any other staff members, not all the things I told you. When I think of it all, it makes me feel stupid and foolish and crazy. I guess crazy is the right word. But you never make me feel those things when I talk with you."

Doctor Moke replied, "Well, one could use the word 'crazy' but it's not the best of words. You did have a mental illness at the time; an illness which is controlled now and which no longer causes you to be a danger to anyone else. Because of the medicine you're taking and the treatment you've received from Doctor Rogers and other staff, you are now considered competent, able to make decisions on your own and to have responsibility for them.

"Let me go back to the things you told me that morning in the jail. I want to expand on the statements you made and to trace their background. I want to take you back to earlier times when these ideas may have started to grow in your mind. Be patient with me and I ask you not to be offended by my searching through your earlier life. Just as it was in the jail interview, whether or not you choose to answer, it is the same today. It is up to you but it is also *for* you and I expect your answers will contribute to your defense at trial.

"I have had several conversations with your husband and on one occasion I spoke to Frank Blair. Things they told me have provided information from the past, information which I will ask you about. My questions are solely based on that information and my own speculations." (Moke almost said 'my suspicions' but decided that word might have meanings for Susan he didn't want to arouse). "Your husband made no suppositions about these events beyond what he told me. And the one time I talked to Frank he just gave me basic events and no details of why they may have occurred. Do you understand all I've just told you, Susan? Do you have any questions before we start?"

Susan replied, "I have no questions. What you've said is clear and acceptable. That morning in the jail I became convinced by your manner as much as your words. I knew I could trust you. I still do and have no doubt my trust will continue."

Doctor Moke continued, "Thank you, Susan. Now let's go back to when you were ten years old. Your current hospital record indicates you were doing well in school, an A+ student for the most part. I believe it was your mid-term report card that was mostly C's and a couple of D's. In speaking with Doctor Rogers about that period you reported you were feeling 'uneasy and frightened' and you were sleeping poorly for a few months. Try to go back in your mind to that time, Susan. I suspect there was something happening that disturbed you. What was going on in your life, with your family, with your friends? Take your time. Think about it before you answer. Any memories from that time?"

As Doctor Moke sat quietly waiting, he thought of their first meeting in the jail and how long he waited for Susan's first words. After two minutes or more (and two minutes is a long time when a person is waiting for someone to answer) Susan said, "That's the time when my father was having problems with the Unions at Seattle Gas and Electric. He used to talk about it at the dinner table and I'd hear him talking to my mother when they were in the kitchen. I remember him saying things like, 'Those Goddamn Communists, they're the ones causing all the trouble. Those bastards are going to ruin the country. They want to take over and the moment they do we can say goodbye to our freedom and our faith. They're stirring up Unions all over the country and some of our workers are joining the Party. They're anti-God, anti-everything that's good and holy.'

"It wasn't like my father to swear or to curse people but he sure went off during that time. Mother used to try to calm him and I could hear her in the kitchen saying things like, 'Try not to get so angry, Olaf. It upsets me and it will upset Susan. And the language you use isn't like you and it's not nice to hear. Certainly Susan shouldn't be hearing you talk that way.'

"I loved my father. He was my hero and I thought he could do no wrong. It was frightening to hear him and the things he was saying were really scary. We had a priest at school who came to our religion class about once a month and I remember him talking about 'the curse of Communism' and how 'the devil was leading the people like sheep to the slaughter.' I couldn't sleep, I couldn't study; all I could think about was the devil and communists. I *felt* something bad was going to happen to us all and it was coming soon.

"Then one day the nun who taught us English at St. Edward's called me aside after class and asked what was bothering me. Sister Barbara had always been nice to me and I felt like I was special to her. I started crying and told her the communists were getting in my head because my father talked so much about them doing the devil's work. I was beginning to hate them and then I thought because hatred is evil I was becoming evil. Sister Barbara told me the communists were causing difficulty in our country but it was not a fight between good and evil. It was more like people just disagreeing with one another and the devil was not involved in it all. She said, 'God still takes care of those who believe in God so don't be afraid. You're one of God's children, Susan dear.' What Sister Barbara said made me feel so much better and it stopped my worrying. She was always a special person in my life at St. Edwards."

Doctor Moke listened intently as Susan talked and again, as in the jail, he took no notes because that might make it less comfortable for Susan to speak freely. He said, "Now I can better understand why you had such a difficult time back then. When someone is ten years old, things adults talk about can often be frightening. It's good Sister Barbara reached out to you. You know, Susan, I think we all need someone to talk to at times. Thanks for telling me about that difficult time in your life.

"I think that's probably enough for today, but there were a few other times in your life when things seemed a little troubling for you. We need to talk about each of them if possible. How about me coming back at the same time tomorrow and we'll look at another one or two? By the way, if it is unsettling for you to go over these times from the past, please let me know. In the next day or two we should have a trial date scheduled and then we'll know what kind of timetable we'll have to cover all this. I wouldn't ask you to do this but the kind of information you gave me today will contribute to my testimony and will help determine the outcome of your trial." Before Doctor Moke left, Susan said she was willing to meet again the following day.

Later that afternoon Moke had a call from Judge Charles. When he answered the call, the judge started with, "Hello, my friend. How is everything going for you? I hope you and Ann are both well. Margaret and I were saying last evening that it's been too long since we had dinner together. I was thinking of trying to arrange a time when we could do just that, but I thought this might not be a favorable time. I plan to set the trial date for Susan Hanson approximately four weeks from today. My calendar is finally opening up. I'll let you know the precise date within the next couple of days.

Having dinner together close to trial date may be perceived by some nosey person as improper, especially since your testimony will possibly be the key to exonerate Ms. Hanson. Will you be ready for your testimony by then?"

Doctor Moke replied, "The timing is good as far as I'm concerned. I have my outline prepared; now I need to fill in a little more information. I have the tree; I just need to give life to the branches. I think you're right to postpone dinner until after the trial. There will probably be a good bit of news media coverage of the trial considering Susan's father was a fairly prominent man in Seattle."

Judge Charles interjected, "I had forgotten all about Olaf Larson. He ran for mayor twenty or thirty years ago. The news media are sure to pick that up and run the story."

Moke said, "So we're agreed to postpone dinner but we'll set a date for dinner once the trial is over." Charles said he'd give Moke the trial date as soon as it was finalized and they'd do dinner within the week after the trial.

The following day Doctor Moke met with Susan Hanson again. He reminded her he was digging into her past to gain material for his court testimony. He opened with, "Today I want to ask you about the time when you were eighteen and about to graduate from St. Edward's High School. Your record here at the hospital has a note by Doctor Rogers stating that a month or two before graduation there was a marked change in your behavior. You quit the volley ball team, you resigned as co-chair of the prom committee, and you quit socializing with friends and classmates. I know from your records your father was running for the office of Mayor of Seattle that year. I realize he was defeated but that didn't occur until months later at election time. Was the fact he was running for office somehow disturbing you? Did that have anything to do with this social withdrawal shortly before graduation?"

Susan sat quietly, apparently deciding how to approach Moke's questions. She finally responded, "I'm not sure it's safe to tell you. Can I really trust you? Oh, never mind, forget I said that. I have to believe I can trust you. If I can't trust you I can't trust anyone. The communists were getting stronger every day and were infiltrating the unions. My father was always supportive of the AFL and other workers' unions, but as the communists' presence became more pronounced and intrusive, my father became increasingly angry and bitter not just about the company he managed but about the whole country. He listened to the news during every meal and cursed off and on about 'those Goddamn reds.' The news was frightening to listen to but so was my father. I began to believe the communists were watching our house and I started being careful about everything I said to anyone. My father said some of his long-time employees were giving the communists confidential information about the company. They were betraying his trust. One night at the dinner table I remember him saying, 'Those Goddamn communists have spies all over. They're listening to us. They're watching us. They're out to destroy us.' Of course, in my mind 'us' included Mother and me.

"The communists were supporting for mayor one of the leaders in the AFL local. Their daily newspaper, *People's Daily World,* began printing scurrilous articles about my father, accusing him of cheating the public and his employees. They nicknamed him 'Lying Larson' and made up all kinds of untruths. After a month or two, father just gave up. He kept working but he quit campaigning. Some of his friends wanted him to sue for libel but I really believe he was afraid of the power of 'The Reds.' I lived in a sad and bitter house. Father would sit for hours with his head in his hands and Mother would try to cheer him up. I was more or less on my own to deal with it. My response was to become increasingly fearful for the three of us.

"I wanted to withdraw from school but my parents were shocked when I even mentioned it. So I did the only thing I could do. I withdrew emotionally. It was so near the end of the term I got by without studying any more. It was a lonely time for me. Father and mother were struggling to keep going and I feared they might not make it. And I lived in fear with the thought, 'what will happen to *us* then.' Father and mother started to attend Mass two or three times during the week in addition to Sunday. To me, that behavior meant 'they are desperate.' I think their faith probably kept them going in spite of their unhappiness and fear. It was a rough time. I don't think they ever fully recovered. Sometimes I wonder if I did.

"I was troubled all those years even to the point of struggling with my own faith. Possibly I remained faithful because I thought the Lord would protect me from satanic communism. My parents both encouraged me to go to college. I hadn't thought much about the future, perhaps because I doubted I would have one. Communism was going to destroy the world, at least the world of Christianity. Strangely, a catholic college seemed at the time to be a haven so I registered at Seattle University with the Jesuits. I'm glad I went there. I felt protected and during that same period of time I met Oscar, as you probably know.

"My father continued to warn everyone he met about communism. It was always the theme when Oscar and I visited my parents. Father died of a stroke eleven years after Oscar and I married. Father always slept late and mother would get up to fix breakfast. One day she came to wake father about nine o'clock and found him dead in the bed. She insisted he was asleep when she got up because she always watched his breathing when she got out of bed. That's how much she worried about him, checking all the time. She insisted someone came in the house and smothered my father while she was in the kitchen fixing breakfast. He had been in good health as far as they knew. My father's doctor told them he was in good health except for mild hypertension, and he was not taking any medicine. After a cursory examination his doctor signed off on the death certificate as a cerebral vascular accident. Of course, there was no basis for an autopsy. I should say my mother was not always thinking clearly in those days. She died a year later of uterine cancer.

"Oscar and I talked about my mother's claim of foul play in my father's death. Oscar said my father talked so often and so fearfully of communism that my mother accepted his fears and lived them herself in their last years together. That may be true but I had reason to believe my father's fears were well founded and I've always half-believed my mother's theory about his death."

Susan grew silent as if she was caught up in the thought she just expressed. Doctor Moke spoke, "Why do you think the communists would be motivated to harm your father, Susan?"

Susan replied, "My father was always out-spoken in his criticism of communism. He saw it as an evil force, a work of the devil. And he said so to everyone he knew. After he discontinued his campaign to be mayor, he was depressed and withdrawn at home. He continued working a few years until his retirement. After he retired he continued going to union meetings, to town hall meetings, to parish meetings, to Knights of Columbus meetings and every other meeting he could find. He spoke vehemently against communism; he was a powerful speaker. He used to say, 'You can't tease the devil.' But you see that's exactly what father was doing. I think 'the devil' was bent on retaliating and the communists were the devil's agents.

"Father listened to the McCarthy hearings on the radio. He bought our first television so he could watch the hearings. He behaved like he was at the meetings. He cheered when McCarthy spoke and he boiled with verbal rants when anyone doubted McCarthy or criticized him in any way. I've sometimes wondered if the force of his frenzies and tirades might have damaged his heart."

After a respectful pause, Doctor Moke asked, "How did all this affect you, Susan?"

Susan replied, "I think you've known the answer to that since the day we first met. The communists never have enough. They want it all. Revenge is the cold heart of the movement. They've wanted me. I was inwardly aware of their intent and on occasion my awareness became overwhelming.

"I'm tired Doctor Moke. It drains me to recall all these things I've talked about although I don't mind talking to you about them. And as you say, 'Sometimes it's good to talk to someone about our thoughts and things that have happened.' But talking today stirs rivers of feelings that run through my life, and I need to get my feet on the shore. The rivers aren't safe."

Doctor Moke replied, "Try to remember what you just said about the rivers and the shore. Keep talking, Susan, because talking is like wading to the shore and will save you from the river. But I agree. I think we've done enough talking for today. Thank you for your openness. Judge Charles called me a couple of days ago. The trial will be in four weeks. The exact date and time is not yet set. By the way, does the attorney, Robert Craven, still visit you?"

"Yes, I see Mr. Craven every two weeks now, usually only for five or ten minutes. He seems to have all he needs to know from me. Can you come back in two days, Doctor Moke? I think I need some time to digest what we talked about today." Doctor Moke said he'd return at their usual time in two days.

Susan appeared anxious when Doctor Moke returned. He noted it but decided not to ask about it. He felt confidant she would confide if she had a concern. Moke began, "Well, here we are again digging into your past. You have been cooperative and quite tolerant of my probing. I appreciate it. The area I want to start off with today is quite personal for you. I hope it won't embarrass you. You know I've talked with Oscar and asked him to fill me in on incidents from the past that might be of value in my testimony. I asked him about this subject and he spoke quite frankly. The subject is birth control. You had been married several years when this became a subject you and Oscar talked about. You were firm in your position that you didn't want to have children. Can you tell me why you made that decision?"

Susan didn't hesitate. "I don't mind talking about it. I was continuing to go to Mass on Sundays and I kept praying that God would destroy Satan-Communism. My church was opposed to birth control except for what they called 'the rhythm method,' avoiding intercourse during fertile periods. That's what I was doing and kept a calendar to be sure when safe-sex was possible. As you probably know, Oscar found the calendar. Then I insisted he use condoms or we maintain the calendar schedule. I felt the presence of Communism was not only invading my life but seducing my mind. Yes, it was more than seductive. It felt like mental rape. Senator McCarthy's hearings convinced me our country would eventually be taken over by Russia because of communist influence and their infiltration in the government, in the movies, in the unions, in the schools, even in the F.B.I. I did not want to bring a child into an evil country.

"Oscar and I began listening to the radio lectures by Monsignor Fulton Sheen in the late forties. He began to present *Life Is Worth Living* in 1951 or 52. We watched him on television and we marveled at his eloquence and his open condemnation of Communism. Then I began to be so frightened by his remarks I thought it best not to listen to him anymore. I would be frightened for days and sleep poorly. In the last lecture I listened to, Sheen concluded it saying, 'Stalin must one day meet his judgment.' Stalin died of a stroke within the week. Sheen talked about Satan's "new church-kingdom" taking over the world and Satan's visible head in Moscow.

"According to the news, Satan's kingdom was growing in China and Korea, everywhere, but especially in America. The trials of Alger Hiss and the Rosenberg's convinced me how active the communists were in America. I was convinced they had spies everywhere and my mind became increasingly convinced they were spying on me, watching my behavior. My father was their target years back when he ran for mayor. Then when he gave speeches against communism they marked him and his family for revenge. I became afraid to listen to Bishop Sheen because "the Reds" would somehow know about it. I was afraid to talk to anyone about my fears because they would *silence me* as they had silenced my father. They killed him!

"That's a long story to let you know why I was completely opposed to bringing a child into this world. If I had become pregnant I would probably have had an abortion in spite of church teaching. I could not bring a helpless child into a place of living hell."

Doctor Moke sat quietly during Susan's remarks. He continued his silence for a short time and then replied, "After all you've said today, and I appreciate the completeness of your answer, I have one important question for you. Think carefully about the question before you answer. And if you're not sure about the answer just let me know. I don't know if you are still of child-bearing age. Let's say that you are. The question is: would you still refuse to have children for the same reason you had in the past?"

Susan was silent and appeared puzzled. She sat looking at her hands and then closed her eyes. Moke noted her avoidance of eye contact and knew she was having a hard time with this one. After a time, she looked at Doctor Moke and said, "I'm having difficulty answering your question. I've not gone through any *what if* thinking recently. Your question confronts a place in me where I'm struggling. I think you know that and I think that's why you asked the question. At the moment I'll answer the question by taking the alternative you allowed: I'm not sure. But your question does lead me to a place I need to go, an island in my mind that needs to be explored. Where does it fit in the rest of my world? Is it a solidly attached piece of my world? Is it a place I need to explore thoughtfully and learn whether or not it is really significant?"

Doctor Moke smiled and said, "I must say, Susan, your remarks often show a remarkable insight, insight I'm not sure you are always aware of, but insight that will continue to assist you in the therapy you're having with Doctor Rogers. Now I have something scheduled in my office so I'm afraid we don't have time to review any additional questions today. Could we meet again the day after tomorrow, same time?" Susan agreed on the meeting time.

When Doctor Moke returned to his office he found two messages, one from Judge Charles who left the message the trial will begin at ten a.m. Thursday of next week. The second was a call from Susan's attorney, Robert Craven, asking him to return the call. He had his secretary get Craven on the line. When they were connected, Mr. Craven said, "Thanks for getting back to me so soon. I presume Judge Charles has given you the information about the trial. I would appreciate it if we could schedule a meeting within the next three or four days so we can go over your trial testimony. I'm sorry I didn't call you once we knew we only had a month before trial. I've been tied up in a complex case the past several weeks which was fortunately just settled. How is your schedule?"

Doctor Moke replied, "I considered calling you but decided you would call when you were ready to meet. Susan told me she was still seeing you for brief visits. I have the impression your visits are reassuring to her. I figured you'd call some day when you were here and stop by, but your recent case probably left you without time. I'm looking at my schedule. I'm meeting with Susan again this Thursday. I'm going over some details with her which I believe will strengthen my testimony. Do you have anything open this Friday, morning or afternoon?"

Mr. Craven said, "Can we make it Friday afternoon at one o'clock? Then I'll see Susan during visiting hours. Do you know when the sheriff will transport her to the jail?"

Moke replied, "The sheriff plans on picking her up next Tuesday morning at ten. I am sending one of our LPN's with Susan in hope of softening her memories of being in jail and make the time there less traumatic. I have the warden's permission for the LPN to accompany her to her cell and remain with her in the cell for at least thirty minutes to help her acclimate."

Craven responded, "Your arrangements for the transfer are very thoughtful, Doctor Moke. Thank you for arranging it. The care Susan has received at the hospital has been excellent. Sending the LPN is an extension of that care. Now my hope is that whatever happens in court we will be able at least to avoid a prison term. I believe prison life would be destructive to Susan and more than she could tolerate."

Moke said, "Yes, prison life would irrevocably bring the demons back into her mind and I doubt anyone could alleviate the results. Let's hope we have jury members who have some appreciation of the complexities of the human mind. I'll expect you at one p.m. this coming Friday."

After the conversation ended, Doctor Moke sat quietly at his desk contemplating the possibilities facing Susan and reviewing his own role as the only witness likely to have an impact on the jury. At this point he didn't know who else Mr. Craven was planning to put on the stand. He would ask on Friday. As he continued thinking about the upcoming trial it occurred to him to enlist Robert Craven's cooperation and be sure Craven called the witnesses who could support Moke's basic argument. He could use their corroborating testimony as background for his own. He decided they'd have to work it out on Friday but the thought also occurred "this is rather late to be getting into this. Craven should have found the time to meet with me much sooner."

The following afternoon Doctor Moke made his visit to Susan at the usual time. He had three items on his list: the Traceys, retirement, and the night before the murder. Of course, he had known the story of the night before the murder since his visit with Susan in the jail. No need to review that. He still had the notes he made after the jail visit. To begin their meeting he told Susan about the trial date and when she would be transported to the Seattle jail. He explained how Marie Murphy, one of the LPN's who worked with her, would be accompanying her to the jail. Susan expressed her gratitude.

Then Doctor Moke began to question her about the material still on his list. "Susan, back in the late forties or early fifties you and Oscar were friends with a couple named Tracey. Oscar told me the two of you used to visit the couple fairly regularly, often having dinner together in each other's homes. He said you suddenly changed your attitude about seeing them and you'd make excuses when he mentioned getting together or if they called to arrange something with you both. Can you recall why that was? Were you offended by something they did or said?"

Susan was thoughtful and closed her eyes remembering. "Yes, I remember Edith and Joe. We enjoyed their company. As I recall they were having dinner at our house and it was the evening when Fulton Sheen gave his weekly lecture. Oscar and I quit listening to Sheen several months before, at my insistence I might add. That evening after dinner we were still sitting at the table talking when Edith mentioned it was time for Sheen's talk and could they watch it with us. There wasn't much we could do but say 'yes'. They knew we had been watching him. So Oscar turned the TV on and brought up the right channel. I knew I couldn't stay in the room. I told them I wasn't feeling well and retired to my room.

"I decided there and then they were not to be trusted. Even though I knew of Edith's claimed allegiance to Sheen, I had an eerie feeling they deliberately continued the after-dinner conversation with us to trick us into listening to Sheen. They wanted to watch my reactions to his criticism of communism. Their apparent devotion to Sheen's lectures and his criticism of "The Red Satan" would be exactly the kind of behavior communist spies would adopt to weave their way into our confidence. I decided they had been working their way into our life since we first knew them. That was the end of my contact with Edith and Joe. While we still lived in that area Oscar used to walk down to their house sometimes and talk to Joe. I never spoke to them again. I wasn't going to let anyone trick me. That was one of the reasons we moved to our present house. Of course, it was also closer to Oscar's work."

Susan seemed to be finished with the subject and Moke was ready to leave it there. Last on his list was her job, so he introduced the subject. "Oscar told me you quit working for Social Security one year before you were due for full retirement. He said you seemed to be in good health at the time and he'd never heard you complain of any problems at work. When Oscar asked you the reason for quitting, you said, 'I can't work with people I can't trust.' And you refused to say anything more about it. Had something happened at work that made you decide you couldn't trust the people who were working with you?"

Susan answered without hesitation, "At least two people in the Social Security office belonged to the communist party. I believe there were several others but they were secretive about it. Those two talked to each other every chance they got and they seemed to avoid the rest of us. I'd see them at the water fountain talking and laughing. My desk wasn't far away and I could hear them talking but couldn't make out what they said. I thought I heard my name a few times. I knew they watched me and when they walked by my desk they looked over my shoulder to see what I was doing. I tried to hide the documents on my desk when they walked by. It made me feel awkward and exposed. One day I just decided I'd had enough. I typed out my resignation, signed it and handed it to my supervisor at the end of the day and left."

Doctor Moke asked, "Did you ever regret the decision, Susan?"

Susan was thoughtful and after a long pause replied, "I've thought about it a lot these past months. Doctor Rogers has helped me think more carefully about making decisions. He encourages me not to decide things on impulse or even on initial consideration. He often says it's important 'to think things over' and sometimes he adds, 'to talk things over with a friend.' Those words are helpful to me and give me pause. I can't say quitting was the best decision I ever made, but Oscar and I still have each other and once this trial is over we'll see what the future holds for the two of us."

Doctor Mock asked, "Are you worried about the trial, Susan?" She replied saying she prays about it every day and asks God to move the jury to do what's right. "What do you think is right, Susan?"

Susan replied, "My mind is not the mind I had that Sunday morning a year ago. That's one thing I'm sure of. It's painful for me to realize I killed a human being, much less a dear friend. Over and over I ask God to decide what's best. I have a hard enough time handling little things. I ask myself what **would** I do if the jury found me innocent? Oh, I'll always know I'm not innocent. But if they find me not guilty, then what? Where will I go? What will I do? How will I live knowing what I've done? I'm sure Oscar will take me back. I know he loves me. I've never doubted his love. I don't understand how he can still love me after what I did. But where would we live? I don't think I could go back to that same house. Oscar continues to live there, but I don't think I could or even that I should. I guess I'll cross the bridge when I know where it leads and make the choices when I get to the other side."

Doctor Moke commented, "Another thoughtful realization on your part, Susan. And by the end of next week I expect you will be on the other side of the bridge. I should warn you the decision may not be entirely yours even if the jury finds you 'Not guilty.' The judge has the prerogative of stipulating conditions that could limit your freedom.

"I'm meeting with your attorney this afternoon to discuss my testimony as well as any recommendations I might have in regard to witnesses. I'll try to stop over Tuesday morning before the sheriff arrives to transport you to the jail. Thanks for your openness in talking with me.

"One other thing and I will discuss this with Mr. Craven this afternoon. We may or may not want you to testify in court. Would it be difficult for you to be in the witness box and respond to questions like the ones I've asked you over the past few weeks? The twelve jurors would be sitting there watching and listening. Would you be frightened? Or embarrassed? Or might you feel sad and get tearful? I don't know if you can really answer the question since you've probably never had that kind of experience. As you know, the jurors would not be allowed to ask you questions, but the prosecuting attorney almost certainly would ask questions and could be hostile and deliberately intimidating."

It was a pleasant relief for Doctor Moke when Susan responded with a smile and the first sign of levity he ever saw in her, "Would the prosecuting attorney's questions be any more intimidating than the ones you've asked, Doctor Moke?"

Moke laughed and replied, "That does my heart good to see some flippancy on your part, Susan. It's good to meet that side of you. It's a good sign if you can find some humor at a time like this."

Susan continued, "I don't think I'd be frightened or easily intimidated by the prosecutor's questions. Both Doctor Rogers and you have helped me become more comfortable in talking to professionals. And you've both helped me clarify my thinking and my ability to verbalize what I want to say." With that ending, Doctor Moke left and went to his office with Mr. Craven's visit next on his calendar.

Robert Craven arrived promptly at one. Doctor Moke was hoping Craven would be less aggressive and more comfortable during this visit. After their greetings, Mr. Craven thanked him for arranging this time to get together. He commented, "I should have come to see you weeks ago but I got tied up in a complicated lawsuit as I mentioned before. Now I find this case on Judge Charles' docket and scheduled for next week.

"I've had a couple of our clerks researching Susan's family history and her adult history. From our research and from my discussions with family members and with Susan we've not found any history of Susan ever being volatile or assaultive in any way. There is no history of legal issues or arrests, not even a traffic ticket. One of our clerks spoke with neighbors and the people she worked with at Social Security. People who knew her there said they were surprised when she left so suddenly. Asked about her demeanor each one said essentially the same thing, 'She was a good worker but 'different.' And no one explained what they meant by 'different.' No one talked about being her friend."

Mr. Craven continued, "Two of my staff checked the places she lived and then interviewed anyone they could find who knew Susan. There was one couple, let me check my notes, yes, here it is: Tracey, Edith and Joe. Edith said they were good friends for several years and then one night when they'd eaten dinner at Susan and Oscar's house, they sat down in the living room to watch Fulton Sheen's *Life Is Worth Living* lecture. Edith told my clerk she thought Susan behaved rather strangely that evening after they left the table. Susan was unwilling to sit down and watch the program. She mumbled something about her health and left the room. Edith called the next morning and thanked Susan for dinner and asked how she was feeling. Susan replied, 'You're welcome' and hung up. She and Susan never spoke to each other again. My clerk wrote down Edith's comment. Here are her words: 'Oscar would wave when he drove by our house if one or both of us were in the yard and if Susan wasn't in the car.' Edith said it was only a few months before Susan and Oscar moved out of the neighborhood.

"Considering how my clerks have fine-combed Susan's past and found nothing other than these two minor things, I have little to offer in defense of her behavior. 'Being different' and 'dropping a friendship without evident motive' are a long way from explaining what appears to be a cold-blooded and deliberate murder.

"So that's where I am with the case and we're less than one week from trial. I hope you might have some helpful thoughts about what I've just told you. Yesterday as I was going over what's been gathered by my office staff, I noted that Susan is here in the hospital on your recommendation to Judge Charles. The record indicates you were the first person Susan talked to after she was arrested. The record simply states, 'Based on testimony provided by Doctor Stephen Moke, testimony revealed to him by the defendant during interview in the District County Jail on this noted date, Susan Hanson will be remanded to the Braceland Psychiatric Institute in Tacoma, Washington until found able to stand trial.'

"So I rest my case Doctor Moke. I need to know what happened during that interview that brought about Susan's hospitalization for almost one year. I was not permitted to read her hospital records and when I asked questions of staff they gave me next to nothing in response. I need to know where to go with this case."

Doctor Moke was paying careful attention to everything Robert Craven was saying. Craven was right, he didn't have anything, *nada*. Doctor Moke began, "Do you mind if I call you Robert? It would make it a little easier to get into the details I'll tell you about. In my mind they almost require less formality." Craven shrugged and mumbled an "okay." Moke continued and gave him some idea of Susan's behavior in the jail-meeting. He carefully presented and explained the pieces he had been putting together these last few weeks, pieces found in Doctor Roger's notes and recently expanded by Moke with Susan's help.

When Moke completed the "case" as he saw it, Robert Craven seemed impressed with the story and its details. He commented, "Wow! We just may come up with an acquittal. You'll need some jurors who aren't significantly prejudiced about your profession. This is your case now. Tell me what you need from me."

Doctor Moke replied, "I think you're going a little too far there. You're the attorney, not me. But there are some witnesses I think you should call. From what I just told you, I think you'll know the questions to ask them. On the other hand, maybe we should go over it again a day or two before the trial. If you decide you want to do that let me know. I'll be available.

"I'd like to have you call Oscar Hanson, of course. I'm sure you have him prepared to fill in and verify much of the history about Susan and about their life together. It will be embarrassing to both of them for you to ask him to explain why they don't have any children. But it is critical testimony.

The other critical areas for you to cover include their relationship with the Traceys, what Susan told her husband about why she quit her job, and the events of the evening before the murder, the events to which I referred a moment ago.

"I think it would be helpful if you can find two or three people who worked with her at Social Security to testify regarding Susan's general demeanor through the years and their understanding of why she quit.

"And finally on my list would be Frank Blair. Frank would be a good witness. He is a fine man with no grudges or hostility over his wife's death. He works here at the hospital, by the way. Frank could testify as to the relationship of the two couples and any thoughts he had about the night they were together before Lucille's death.

"Something else just occurred to me and you might give this some thought. It might be a good idea to put Dr. Rogers on the stand and ask him general questions about Susan's care as a patient, his treatment and her course in hospital. How has she responded to him? How much improvement has he seen and in what ways has she improved? There is one question I'm not sure about. What do you think? Should you ask him, 'If Susan Hanson is acquitted on all charges today, do you believe it would be safe for her to be totally released from the hospital or would you place any treatment restrictions on her?'"

Mr. Craven attended to everything Dr. Moke was saying and made several notes. He commented, "You're being very helpful and I can't tell you how grateful I am for the work you've done. You have weaved all of this into a sound and sturdy cloth which covers it well; I don't see any holes in it at the moment. Your question about Dr. Rogers's testimony is worth considering. Of course, I'd need to know what his testimony would be. If he's going to recommend continued care either in the hospital or out, it could play a part in the jury deliberations. If there is a recommendation for continued care, it offers a safeguard for the jury to consider."

Moke said, "Let me see if Doctor Rogers is available. If he is, I'll ask him to join us for a short time and we'll get his thinking on it." Moke called the operator and asked her to find Doctor Rogers and have him call Doctor Moke. Within a few minutes Rogers called and Moke said to him, "If you're not busy with someone, could you come to my office? Susan's attorney is here and wants to ask you something about the trial." Rogers said he'd be right over.

When Doctor Rogers arrived and after introductions, Mr. Craven asked him, "I'm considering asking you to testify regarding Ms. Hanson's general care in Braceland Psychiatric Hospital, how cooperative she has been and how responsive she's been to your treatment. I'll ask if she has improved and depending on your answer I may ask you questions about significant signs of her improvement. Doctor Moke and I have been discussing all of this and we're considering whether or not to ask you the following question. If Susan Hanson were acquitted today would you recommend she have further treatment prior to leaving the hospital or would you consider her to be in a condition ready for discharge immediately? If I asked you that question, how would you respond?"

Doctor Rogers closed his eyes in thought. Moke had often seen that same eye pattern of his. After a short time, he opened his eyes and replied, "I certainly wouldn't recommend immediate discharge. The effect of being on trial, the anxious hours spent in the courtroom and hearing all the testimony are bound to be disturbing to her mental and emotional state. I would recommend she return to the hospital after the trial no matter what the outcome. Even if she is sentenced to time in prison I believe she should return to Braceland Psychiatric for some brief evaluation and stabilization prior to going to prison. If she is found innocent, I would recommend she return to Braceland and remain for a period of time and be reevaluated prior to release. When released, I would anticipate recommending she continue treatment and medication as recommended by her treating physician."

Moke gave Craven a questioning look and waited for his comment. It wasn't long in coming. "Doctor Rogers, your testimony as you state it could only be helpful. If I ask you to testify, before you leave the witness chair I'll ask that last question and you can give the answer pretty much as you just stated it. Depending on how the trial is going, it's possible that's the only question I will ask you. Thanks for coming over. I think that's all I need from you today." After Doctor Rogers left, the Superintendent and the attorney chatted a bit and agreed to make contact if anything else came up for either of them. Just before Mr. Craven left, Moke suggested if Craven could find Sister Barbara still around at St. Edward's Grade School, she might be a good witness. Craven responded, "I'll try. Nuns usually make impressive witnesses." Now it was countdown time to the trial.

When he got home that evening, as was his pattern, Stephen made a Southern Comfort Manhattan for Ann and himself and the two of them sat and discussed their day. Ann always had dinner prepared. It was only a question of when to put it in the oven. They might talk for fifteen minutes or it might be forty-five. When they were first married they made a pact that neither would come to the dinner table with an unshared burden from the day.

As they talked before diner Stephen mentioned Susan Hanson's trial was scheduled for the following week. He was thoughtful for a moment and said, "Ann, you and I both believe in divine providence. We've talked about it many times and have often remarked how so many things seem almost to be preordained. I can't help but wonder what would have happened to Susan Hanson if I had not been the one to interview her in her cell?"

Ann responded, "I can't believe it would have turned out differently in the end. From what you've told me, Susan has a good chance of being acquitted. If she is truly innocent, I believe it would have worked out in some other way without your interview or testimony. If she is truly innocent in the eyes of the law, God would have found another way for her to be exonerated. On the other hand, we both know some people are in prison and are later proven to be innocent of the crime. So much in life is mystery."

Stephen replied, "I certainly agree with your last comment, Love. We live as if our lives will follow the plans we make. Sometimes they do, sometimes they don't. Chance or providence? We'll never know, will we?" As Ann headed for the kitchen, Stephen heard her say, "someday we will!" They ate slowly and moved to discussing the news of the day.

The few days left before the trial went quickly. On Monday the sheriff's office gave the Braceland Institute notice a car would arrive at ten a.m. the following morning to transport Susan Hanson to the Seattle Municipal Jail, Hanson to be accompanied by one Institute employee. On Tuesday morning Doctor Moke went to Building #3 and talked briefly with Susan. He told her he was confident she would conduct herself well not only in the court but also during the few days in jail. He said he expected the trial would not last more than two or three days. He expressed the hope she would be exonerated and told her he was praying for her and for a favorable outcome at the trial. Susan gave him her hand as she had the day he interviewed her in the jail. She smiled with the unexpressed memory they shared.

Mr. Craven called Doctor Moke Tuesday afternoon to ask if they could get together Wednesday morning to review his choice of witnesses and the order in which he planned to have them testify. They agreed on ten a.m. in Moke's office.

The following day Mr. Craven came to Moke's office at ten a.m. with his list of witnesses. They drifted into a first name basis for the discussion. Stephen suggested they consider the witnesses in relation to the development of the basic story. Robert agreed but thought they should introduce some background about Susan's family. Stephen said, "Yes, of course. I suppose Oscar would be the most likely one to provide that. Susan has no siblings or other close relatives to provide it." They agreed to use Oscar to provide some family background with focus on Olaf, Susan's father, and his position as Director of Seattle Gas and Electric. Oscar would also testify as to the death of Olaf and his wife's attitude about Olaf's death. Oscar had personal knowledge of this information.

They went through Robert's list of witnesses one by one and agreed this was a suitable way to present the evidence that would then be brought together and clarified by Doctor Moke's testimony. Doctor Rogers would be the final witness for the defense.

Stephen summed up their meeting, "It looks to me like you have it arranged very well. You did a thorough job getting the school reports and lining up the Traceys and the two women from the Social Security Office. I'm sure you have primed Doctor Rogers for his testimony. I guess this covers everything. I'll see you in court Thursday morning."

Robert answered, "Thanks for working with me on this, Stephen. Actually I'll be in court this afternoon. The Judge has scheduled jury selection at two p.m. today. Anything I should be looking for in the *voir dire?*"

Stephen thought for a while and then replied, "Try to forget you're an attorney when each person is called up. Imagine you have a company and you're hiring a new person with whom you will be working closely, discussing plans, maybe having lunch on occasion. How does it *feel?* If the person doesn't feel right, raise your usual questions. If you don't come up with cause for dismissal, do a peremptory challenge and get rid of them. But whatever the outcome of the trial is, don't blame me. You can blame yourself for taking my inadequate advice. Now you better get on the road for Seattle." Robert thanked Stephen again and left the office.

Doctor Moke called Ann and asked if she would like to come by for lunch in his office. While they were eating Ann mentioned she had a call from Margaret Thomas that morning. "Margaret asked if I planned on coming to Seattle for the trial. When I said I was coming up with you, she asked me to stop at her house and the two of us will go to the trial together and we'll have lunch and do some visiting. You'll be occupied during the lunch break with Mr. Craven and Doctor Rogers. So you can drop me at their house in Bothell on the way."

Stephen replied, "That's a great arrangement. It will be much better for you to be with someone during the trial. You have afore-knowledge at least about my testimony. You've heard the story from the very beginning and you've agreed the pieces fit together well, so you can just follow along."

Stephen and Ann left at eight the following morning. He dropped Ann at the Thomas home and waited until Margaret opened the door before driving away. He arrived at the courthouse about nine-fifteen. He saw Doctor Rogers and suggested they go have coffee at a spot nearby. On the way they met Robert Craven who joined them. They watched the time as they chatted about the weather and their varied arrival times. Stephen asked Robert how the *voir* dire went on Wednesday. Robert replied, "It went well but I did use the preemptory challenge once. He looked and sounded like a man who would have problems getting along with anyone. By the way, since you and I talked, Stephen, I've found a surprise witness. I visited the religious community still teaching at St. Edward's School. Sister Barbara is retired but still living in the convent. She remembered Susan well and remembered the special conversation they had when Susan was in fourth grade. I plan to put Sr. Margaret on the stand right after I dismiss Oscar Hanson the first time."

Moke replied, "That's great. She will be a good witness. A nun on the stand should impress the jury and her testimony will get our defense story off to a good start. Nice work, Robert."

They were back in the courthouse by nine-fifty and went directly into the court room. Mr. Craven's clerk sat beside him. A seat was then saved for the defendant. Doctor Moke sat next to the empty seat at the defense table. Doctor Rogers sat behind Mr. Craven. Two guards brought Susan Hanson into the court room and seated her next to Mr. Craven's law clerk. At promptly nine o'clock the Honorable Charles Thomas entered as the bailiff announced, "Hear ye, hear ye, All stand for the Honorable Charles Thomas." Judge Thomas sat at the bench and after going through the preliminaries, he looked at Susan Hanson and said, "Susan Hanson, you are charged with first degree murder in the death of Lucille Blair. How do you plead?"

Robert Craven stood and responded, "Not guilty, your Honor."

Judge Thomas turned to the Prosecutor, who had previously stated her name as Janet Wilson, and said, "Ms. Wilson present your case for the prosecution."

Janet Wilson rose and began, "I call to the stand, Sergeant Michael Brown." After Officer Brown was sworn in by the court clerk, Ms. Wilson asked his name, rank and unit. She continued, "And were you on duty the morning of March tenth nineteen hundred and sixty-six." He replied in the affirmative. Questioning continued, "You were called to the address of 5294 Hill Street in Seattle?" Another affirmative. "Tell the jury what you saw when you arrived at that address."

Officer Brown replied, "There was a woman standing on the porch of the house with a butcher knife in her hand. There was blood on the knife. Another woman with a bleeding wound in her upper abdomen was lying on the porch near the woman with the knife. There was a pool of blood by her body. I checked for a pulse. She was dead. There was a man on the porch sobbing and obviously distraught. He said he was the dead woman's husband and he was the one who called the police. As we spoke, another man came from across the street and was obviously horrified by the scene. When he saw the knife in the woman's hand and the other woman dead at her feet, he said, 'Susan, good God, what have you done to Lucille?' Before we left I asked this man's name. It was Oscar Hanson; he was the husband of the woman with the knife. My partner called for an ambulance but when they arrived they didn't touch the body since the woman was dead. We called for an investigating team. The ambulance crew remained at the scene as my partner and I took the woman who held the knife to the district jail. Before we left I put on gloves and took the knife from her hand and laid it on the porch. I needed almost to pry the knife from her fingers."

Gloria Wilson was ready with her next question, "Sergeant Brown, did you note anything unusual about the prisoner?"

Craven was on his feet. "Objection." Judge Charles asked what the objection was. Craven: "'Anything unusual' calls for an assessment of the prisoner, an assessment Sergeant Brown is unable to make." "Overruled" came from the bench. Gloria Wilson told Brown to answer the question.

The sergeant replied, "The prisoner never spoke a word, on the porch, in the car or as we booked her in the district jail. Two days later I was on jail duty and escorted the prisoner to Judge Charles's court for arraignment. She never spoke to me and never opened her mouth to the judge or anyone else. I believe she continued in silence for several days. In my mind that behavior was unusual."

Ms. Wilson said, "This is our only witness. Let me point out to the jury that the defendant was transferred to the Braceland Psychiatric Institute within a few days of being arrested and has been there until two days ago when she was returned to jail pending this trial. The state rests."

The judge turned to Mr. Craven who said, "No cross. The defense calls to the stand Oscar Hanson." Sworn in by the court clerk, Oscar took the stand. Craven began, "Tell the jury: what is your relationship to the prisoner and the extent of that relationship and please include what information you have about the immediate family of the accused."

"Susan Hanson is my wife. She is the only child of Olaf and Florence Olson. We were married in 1944, the year Susan graduated from Seattle University. We met at a parish function and began dating when Susan was in her junior year. I knew her parents well. Her father became the Director of Seattle Gas and Electric. He ran for mayor in 1940 but was defeated. At that time members of the communist party became active in the unions and in politics. Her father died in 1950 and her mother died two years later."

Mr. Craven, "How did Mr. Olsen, Susan's father, die and how did Mrs. Olsen respond to his death?"

Mr. Hanson, "Mr. Olsen was found dead in bed one morning. Mrs. Olsen said he was breathing when she got out of bed to prepare breakfast. When she returned a little later, he was dead. She always insisted communists found their way into the house and smothered him. She held onto that belief until the time of her death. I was never sure but I always thought Susan possibly believed her mother's story."

Mr. Craven, "I believe you spent a good bit of time with Susan's parents while they were still alive. Do you remember any stories they told about Susan when she was young?"

Mr. Hanson, "Oh yes, I remember lots of stories. Olaf was quite a talker. They often talked about how quiet Susan was and how easily she became frightened. She never liked to have people in the house who weren't relatives or good friends of the family. She was a good student apparently and made friends at school after an initial reticence. There was a difficult time in, I think it was fourth grade, when they thought she was ill. It went on for several months. She was withdrawn, seemed very anxious, was sleeping poorly and doing badly in school. Then it suddenly cleared up and she was back to her usual self.

"The same sort of thing happened in her senior year of high school. Actually she wanted to quit school at that time but her parents wouldn't permit it. She withdrew from sports and from school activities. She was involved in planning the senior dance but she withdrew from it and didn't even go to the dance. If she hadn't had good grades, it was quite possible she might not have graduated. Whatever it was, they said things got better in the summer and Susan enrolled at Seattle University for the fall semester. When I happened to be alone with her mother, she would sometimes quietly say to me, 'I worry about Susan. She gets suspicious of people at times and seems to have hidden fears she's never willing to talk about.'"

Mr. Craven, "Have you ever had concerns like her mother mentioned?"

Mr. Hanson, "I have sometimes wondered why Susan made some of the decisions she made. If I asked Susan why she made a particular decision, she never really explained it, at least to my satisfaction. She'd say a few words and I learned there was no use in asking again. It would only irritate her. I'm not suggesting she was difficult to get along with. She was a good wife and we got along well. When I'd mention things like this to a couple of friends at work, they'd usually say something like 'that's how women are. Get used to it.' And I got used to it; so there was never really a problem between us."

Mr. Craven, "Thank you for your testimony, Mr. Hanson. I wish to dismiss Mr. Hanson at this time but reserve the right to recall him to the stand at a later time."

The Judge asked the prosecutor if she wanted to cross examine Mr. Hanson regarding the testimony he had given. She replied, "Not at this time, your honor." Mr. Hanson was excused.

Mr. Craven, "I now call to the stand Sister Margaret." Sister Margaret was sworn in and took the stand. Mr. Craven continued, "Please, state your full name, your current work, and your relationship with Susan Hanson, the accused."

The witness replied, "I'm Sister Margaret Donovan, a member of the Daughters of Charity who teach at St. Edward's Grade and High School in Seattle. I am currently retired. I first met Susan Hanson (her last name was Olsen at the time) when she was in my fourth grade class at St. Edwards. I would occasionally catch sight of her and wave or say hello during the following years she was in our school. We've had no contact since she left St. Edwards."

Mr. Craven: "Please tell the members of the jury about Susan's year in your class room, what kind of student she was, any difficulties that occurred during the year, and any specific conversations or interactions you remember having with her during that fourth grade year."

Sister Margaret, "Susan was a good student and friendly toward her classmates. She got along well with everyone but I couldn't say she had a 'best friend' as youngsters that age say. I really didn't have favorites and I was interested in all the children in my class, but Susan seemed special in a way. There came a time when she seemed to change. She looked worried and was not responding in class the way she usually did. She never raised her hand when I asked a question in class and I'd see her standing alone during recess. Her homework wasn't done well and sometimes not at all.

One day during recess I found her standing by herself near the school building. I went over and spoke to her. She responded half-heartedly. I asked her if anything was the matter. She said, and these may not be her exact words, 'I think the devil is in my soul. I'm afraid of the communists because they are working for the devil and planning to take over the world. I hate them and wish they would all die. It's a sin for me to hate that way. So the devil is taking over my soul too.' The poor child looked up at me with tears in her eyes and said, 'What can I do Sister Margaret?' I wanted to hug her but thought it wasn't appropriate so I took her hands and held them in mine and said, 'Dear little Susan, hating things that are evil is not a sin. That puts you on God's side. Don't be frightened. People talk a lot about Communism these days. But God is more powerful than the communists and the devil combined. And remember you're on God's side and God loves you. You're one of God's children.'

"Susan thanked me and ran off to find her friends. Grades improved and she returned to her usual active participation. We never talked like that again, but Susan would always wave and say 'Hi, Sister Margaret' when she saw me. I always felt grateful for the little chat we had and it was such a delight to see her playing with the others and responding in class. I prayed for all my students but especially for Susan."

Mr. Craven, "Thank you for your testimony, Sister Margaret, and thank you for gracing us with your presence today. I hope you return to a long and peaceful retirement."

Before the judge asked, Ms. Wilson said, "No cross." Judge Charles asked Mr. Craven to present his next witness.

Mr. Craven, "I call Edith Tracey to the stand." Edith was sworn in and went to the witness box. Mr. Craven continued, "Please state you name and tell the jury about your relationship with Susan Hanson."

Edith Tracey began, "My name is Edith Tracey. Susan Hanson and her husband were neighbors of ours, (my husband, Mel, and me) for almost six years. The four of us had dinner together quite regularly, usually on Sunday evenings." Edith Tracey went on to describe what happened on a particular Sunday evening when Susan became "unfriendly and aloof" toward Mel and Edith.

When Ms. Tracey finished her statement, Mr. Craven asked, "What was the last contact you had with Ms. Hanson?"

"I called Susan the next day and thanked her for having us to dinner. She replied abruptly with a curt 'Thank you' and she hung up the phone. I've had no contact of any kind since that time."

Craven said, "Nothing further from this witness." "No cross" came from Ms. Wilson.

Judge Charles said, "The witness is dismissed. Perhaps this would be a good time to have a recess. We can all find lunch somewhere. Unfortunately, I can make no particular recommendations since I am an officer of the court. But I can wish you *Bon Appe'tit*. Court will resume promptly at one-thirty."

The officers came immediately to escort Susan back to the court house holding room. Mr. Craven, Doctor Moke and Doctor Rogers agreed to have lunch together. They talked about the trial and all agreed they thought it was going well. Doctor Moke said to Craven, "Robert, that was a great idea to have Sister Margaret testify. She was so convincing and so sincere. One could easily picture her assuring the little ten-year-old that God would take care of her. Her religious habit alone became a focus for the jury but her charm and simplicity was a winner."

Robert said, "Stephen, you might consider high-lighting that scene in your testimony. I think it appealed to the compassion of everyone in the room."

All returned to the courtroom and the guards brought Susan back in at exactly one-thirty. Judge Charles came in with the usual call "Hear ye, hear ye" from the court clerk. The judge was seated and said, "Present your next witness, Mr. Craven."

Mr. Craven: "At this time I ask Mr. Oscar Hanson to return to the stand. Since you've already been sworn in Mr. Hanson, you may go directly to the witness box." When Mr. Hanson was seated, Mr. Craven said, "You have been introduced to the court and to the jury so we will go directly to further testimony. Mr. Hanson, were you and your wife on good terms with your wife's parents, Olaf and Florence Olson and did you visit them often?"

Mr. Hanson: "Yes, we were on good terms and we must have seen them at least once each week as long as they lived. We frequently went to Sunday Mass with them at St. Patrick's church and we often went out to lunch together after Mass. About once a week we stopped by their house to say hello and when we went shopping in the specialty stores we'd go by and ask if they needed anything. They were both very fond of Susan as their only child, and I'm sure they were fond of me."

Mr. Craven: "Thank you, Mr. Hanson. Your honor I wish to submit Exhibit A, a transcript of the St. Patrick's High School record for the senior class year of Susan Olson, now Susan Hanson. I will ask Mr. Hanson if this information is familiar to him."

The court clerk showed the exhibit to the Judge and then to the State's Attorney. The Judge said, "Without objection the exhibit is accepted. The clerk may show the exhibit to the jurors and to the witness for his testimony."

Mr. Craven: "Mr. Hanson, is the information on this transcript a surprise to you or is it in keeping with the information you received from Susan's parents regarding her senior year in high school, information which you have just related to the jury?"

Mr. Hanson: "This transcript agrees with the knowledge I had from Susan's parents regarding her senior year."

Mr. Craven: "Thank you Mr. Hanson. Now I'd like to go to another matter, perhaps more serious, and certainly more sensitive. Do you and your wife have any children?"

Mr. Hanson: "No, we do not." Mr. Craven went on to ask him if he and his wife wanted to have children. Hanson replied, "I *thought* we both wanted children. We agreed we did but then I accidently discovered my wife was avoiding pregnancy using the calendar method."

Mr. Craven asked, "When you discovered this, did you ask your wife about it? And if you did, what explanation did your wife have for not wanting children?"

Mr. Hanson replied, "Yes, we talked about it. Susan told me she believed the Communists were taking over one country after another and she believed America was next on their list. She insisted we continue using birth control and said if she got pregnant she would plan to have an abortion. She would not bring a child into a world where in her words 'the Devil will rule.'"

Mr. Craven said, "Thank you, Mr. Hanson. Now let me briefly refer to Edith Tracey and the testimony she gave before we all went to lunch. Were you good friends and did you see them often?"

Mr. Hanson: "Yes, we were very good friends and saw them quite regularly as Ms. Tracy stated. On the evening Ms. Tracey referred to, I thought we were having a good evening but suddenly Susan seemed unwilling to be part of it. I think she used 'not feeling well' as an excuse to leave the room. After they left Susan came out of the bedroom apparently fine and the rest of the evening passed without mention of the Traceys. After that evening Susan always made excuses when I mentioned getting together with the Traceys. I used to walk down and talk to Joe when he was out in the yard and Edith would sometimes come out and visit a bit. But Susan never spoke to either of them again. We moved from the area a couple of years later. Susan was relieved and happy over the move."

Mr. Craven: "Thank you, Mr. Hanson. I have one other area I'd like to ask you about. Tell me about Susan's work, her career if you will."

Mr. Hanson: "Shortly after she finished college Susan became a Case Worker for the Social Security Administration. It was probably about six months after her graduation. During that six months we married and spent the time settling in our first house. Through her working years she never complained about the job or the people with whom she worked. In fact, she rarely said much of anything about the agency or what she did. Then one day when I got home from work, I asked how her day went, which I always asked even though I knew the typical one-word answer, 'good' or 'fine.' But this day the answer to my question about her day was, 'I quit the job.' That was a big surprise. We had never talked about her retiring. I had no idea she even thought about it. My immediate question was 'why?' It wasn't meant as a confrontation or as a request for an explanation. It was just a 'why?'

"Her response was, 'I can't work for people I can't trust.' And that was the end of it. She never elaborated and I really didn't expect her to. That's how Susan was and is. She says what she wants to say in situations, and that's the end of it. We can have great conversations with her whole-hearted participation; but she has a private world which is hers alone."

Mr. Craven: "Thank you again Oscar. Thank you for the breadth of testimony you have given the jury today. You've presented a clear view of Susan in the life you share and have shared for many years. And I believe your testimony has been and will be a great help to the jury in their deliberations. I will not expect to recall you to the witness stand but I will still reserve the right to do so in case other testimony makes it necessary."

Gloria Wilson: "No Cross." And Judge Charles told Mr. Craven to call his next witness. He called Janet Lanigan to the stand. She was sworn in and took the stand.

Mr. Craven: "Ms. Lanigan, please, state your full name and tell us where you work and under what circumstances you know the defendant."

Ms. Lanigan: "My name is Janet Ruth Lanigan. I work for the Social Security Administration and I'm in charge of the Regional Application Office. Susan Hanson was an employee of that office and I was her supervisor after I took the position fifteen years ago and until the time of her resigning two years ago. I can give you the exact dates if necessary."

Mr. Craven: "The dates are not necessary. You were her superior for many years. Can you tell us how you would rate her as an employee on a scale of five? Did she arrive on time for work and complete the expected day? How did she get along with other employees? Did you have any complaints from clients or others outside the work setting?"

Ms. Lanigan: "I would rate Susan's work as a five on a scale of one to five. She did her work on time and it was done well. She kept her scheduled hours and spent her time at work doing her work. She didn't waste time visiting with others. To my knowledge any relationships she had with other's in the office were not extended beyond office hours. She was a good employee and I was surprised and disappointed when she handed in her resignation."

Mr. Craven: "Did Ms. Hanson give you any reason for her resignation?"

Ms. Lanigan: "She did not. She simply stated in her letter, which I have here and I quote: 'I wish to resign at the end of my shift this date from my position in the Regional Application Office of the Social Security Administration.' The letter was addressed to me. When she handed it to me she extended her hand and said, 'Goodbye.' She left before I could respond in any way other than a quick 'Goodbye'. She took nothing from her desk and I felt certain she had no personal things at or on or in her desk. She was very private."

Mr. Craven: "Thank you for your testimony, Ms. Lanigan. I have no further questions."

After the "No Cross" from Ms. Wilson, Judge Charles asked Mr. Craven to call his next witness. He called Jean Ritter.

Ms. Ritter was sworn in and took the stand. Mr. Craven said, "Please, tell the jury your full name and under what circumstance you know the accused, Ms. Susan Hanson."

Ms. Ritter: "My name is Jean Barbara Ritter. I am an employee of the Regional Application Office of the Social Security Administration. I am acquainted with Ms. Hanson because we worked in the same office and my desk was two cubicles from hers."

Mr. Craven: "Did you ever spend time with Ms. Hanson outside the office and did you ever have any personal conversations with Ms. Hanson in the office? From the contacts you had with her can you give the jury your impression of her general behavior? Have you ever seen her angry and do you think she could become violent?"

Ms. Wilson: "Objection to the last question, Your Honor. It calls for speculation." Judge Charles said the objection was sustained and should not be answered.

Ms. Ritter replied to Mr. Craven: "I never talked to or had any contact with Ms. Hanson outside of the office. We had no personal conversations in the office. Ms. Wilson kept busy with her work and from my casual observation it appeared she had minimal interaction with other employees."

Mr. Craven, "Thank you, Ms. Ritter, for your willingness to come and provide testimony today."

After the "No cross" from Ms. Wilson, Ms. Ritter was dismissed by Judge Charles who then suggested all in the court take a twenty-minute break and return promptly at three forty-five. Mr. Craven, Doctor Rogers and Doctor Moke agreed to stay with Ms. Hanson during the break, each of them taking five or ten minutes for necessities. Doctor Moke found a female officer who agreed to accompany Susan to a ladies' bathroom.

By three forty-five all were back in the court room and Judge Charles asked the defense to call their next witness. Mr. Craven called Oscar Hanson back to the stand. Mr. Craven said: "Ladies and gentlemen of the jury, you remember Mr. Hanson's testimony earlier today. Now I have only a few additional questions. Mr. Hanson, you and your wife were out to dinner with Frank and Lucille Blair the night before Lucille Blair's death."

Oscar said a 'yes' and Mr. Craven continued, "Do you recall anything strange about that evening? Any unusual behavior?"

Ms. Wilson: "Objection. Calls for speculation."

Judge Craven thought for a few moments, then replied, "Objection denied. A husband may well have the ability to speculate with accuracy about his wife's behavior."

Mr. Craven: "Thank you, your Honor. Please answer the question, Mr. Hanson."

Mr. Hanson: "When we were at the table, Lucille excused herself and went to the ladies' room. After she returned Susan seemed to become quiet and participated little in our continued conversation. I thought she might have been annoyed because Lucille didn't ask her if she wanted to accompany Lucille to the ladies' room. Later when we got home, Susan said, 'When Lucille went to the ladies' room I wonder why she stopped to talk to that couple at one of the tables when she returned.' She made a similar comment about Lucille after we got in bed that night. I said I never noticed, or something like that. It didn't seem important."

Mr. Craven: "Thank you Mr. Hanson. You will be dismissed if there is no cross examination. Wilson: "no cross." Judge Charles: "Mr. Hanson is dismissed and you may call your next witness."

Mr. Craven: "I call Frank Blair to the stand." Mr. Blair was sworn in and took the stand. Craven continued: "Please state your full name and tell us your relationship to the accused."

Mr. Blair: "My name is Francis John Blair. I am the husband of the deceased, Lucille Blair. Lucille and I were close friends of Oscar and Susan Hanson for the past five years. We lived across the street from them and we frequently went out to dinner with them."

Mr. Craven: "Were you out to dinner with them the night before your wife was killed?"

Mr. Blair: "Yes, we were out to dinner together and ate at Harrah's Casino." Mr. Craven asked if there was anything unusual about the evening. Mr. Blair continued, "It was a pleasant evening. I thought Susan became rather quiet toward the end of dinner but that was not really unusual for Susan. I'd seen it happen before. There was one other thing which was really irregular. I had driven that evening and we always sat as couples in the car. I drove that night. When we approached the car to go home, Susan said, 'Let Lucille ride in the back with me so I can keep an eye on her.' Susan laughed a little, making light of it, but Lucille did sit in the back with Susan."

Mr. Craven, "Were those her exact words, Mr. Blair." Mr. Blair responded with a "yes." And Mr. Craven continued, "Thank you, Mr. Blair. I have no further testimony from this witness."

"No cross" and "This witness is dismissed" came in sequence followed by "Call your next witness, Mr. Craven."

Mr. Craven addressed the Judge: "Your Honor, if it please the court, my next witness will be Doctor Stephen Moke. In view of the time, four-thirty-five, I request the defense be allowed to present the next witness's complete testimony as a whole and not on separate days. It is important for the members of the jury to hear all of his testimony at one time. It is sequentially aligned with the testimony of the witnesses the defense presented today. I believe it is a critical matter for the proper defense of Susan Hanson."

Judge Charles took some time considering the request. Then he addressed the jury, "Ladies and gentlemen of the jury, you have heard Mr. Craven's request. I think it is important that we look favorably on his request. We do want a fair trial and Mr. Craven's petition supports that end. The jury will be dismissed until nine-thirty tomorrow morning. You may return home at this time. I instruct you not to listen to or read news about this trial and I enjoin on you the responsibility not to discuss the case with anyone else or with one another. We will see you promptly tomorrow morning at nine-thirty. The jury is dismissed."

As Dr. Moke was leaving the courtroom he found Ann waiting in the corridor. He said to her, "In my preoccupation with the trial the possibility of staying over never occurred to me. I guess we'll just drive home since we're not prepared to spend the night here. It's only a forty-minute drive, maybe more with afternoon traffic."

Ann smiled and said, "Sweetheart, I was paying close attention to details. I packed a bag with underwear, a change of shirts for you, my cosmetics of course, and both our needed toiletries." When Stephen asked how it was he never saw them in the car, Ann replied, "I packed them and put the bag in the trunk while you were deciding which tie to wear. In the end you wore the one I suggested earlier this morning."

Stephen said, "How come you influence my behavior without my even being aware of it? I'm going to have to pay closer attention to what you're doing."

Ann said, "You'll have nothing to lose. And by the way, Margaret asked me if we would stay at their house. She said it would probably not be a good idea if we went out to dinner because of nosey people seeing us while the trial is still on. She has plenty of food possibilities at their house and she'll be happy to fix dinner for the four of us."

Stephen replied, "That's fine with me. We must remember the Judge's admonition to the jury and I'm sure Thomas will automatically apply that to the four of us. Besides I've had courtroom enough for the day."

Stephen and Ann spent a pleasant evening with Margaret and Thomas talking mostly about politics and the Cold War with Russia. Stephen's mind wandered to the courtroom in silent moments. He felt well prepared for his testimony but he had limited experience in testifying. His biggest concern was naturally the cross examination. He had concern the prosecutor might challenge the domain of psychiatry. If she belittled the field of psychiatry, he might get defensive and show some irritation. Knowledgeable professionals should have respect for his profession. But some of them were surprisingly ignorant and treated mental illness as nothing but an excuse for weakness, ignorance, laziness or even crime.

The next morning Margaret had a healthy breakfast for them all; and as they ate they chatted about the morning's national news. Ann packed the few things they brought and put them in the car. They left at the same time to arrive at the courtroom of the man who became Judge Thomas Charles again.

The jury was seated and all were in the courtroom by nine-thirty when Judge Charles entered with the usual introduction: "Hear Ye, Hear Ye, the Honorable Thomas Charles, please stand." Judge Charles was seated and checked to see if the members of the jury were all present. He said, "Good morning, Ladies and Gentlemen of the Jury. I trust you had a good night and slept well. We need you to be alert and attentive today because we anticipate the outcome of this trial will be given to you to decide before the day's end.

"Mr. Craven, call your next witness."

Mr. Craven called Doctor Stephen Moke to the stand. After Doctor Moke was sworn in and on the stand, Mr. Craven began, "Please state your full name, your credentials and describe your relationship with the defendant."

Doctor Moke: "My full name is Stephen Mock (no middle name or initial). I am a Board Certified Psychiatrist and currently the Superintendent of the Braceland Psychiatric Institute in Tacoma, Washington. I first met Susan Hanson the fourth day after the day she was arrested for the murder of Lucille Frank. I visited her in the City Jail at the request of the Honorable Thomas Charles. At that time and after a lengthy reluctance to even speak, Susan Hanson told me a bizarre and almost incredible story which I have only come to understand fully in the past few months. On the basis of that interview in the jail I recommended to Judge Thomas Charles that Susan Hanson be hospitalized in the Braceland Psychiatric Institute for further evaluation and if necessary for treatment until able to understand the nature of the charges against her and able to cooperate with her attorney in her own defense.

"As a result of my recommendation Susan Hanson was transferred to the Braceland Psychiatric Institute the following week and she has been a patient in that facility until she was temporarily transferred three days ago to the City Jail to stand trial for the murder of Lucille Blair. Her treating psychiatrist at the Braceland Institute was Dr. Ralph Rogers, who is seated behind Mr. Craven.

"I maintained contact with Susan Hanson during her hospitalization this past year. I did that in order to preserve the relationship that developed at the time of our first contact and to maintain my role as an interviewing presence. During the past six or seven weeks and in preparation for this testimony I have spent several evaluative interviews with Ms. Hanson. I have traced the track of fear based on childhood experiences, secretly and persistently spreading inside this girl's mind, a fear growing stronger and more dangerous through the passing years. Initially it was but a weak mental impression but it developed into a controlling influence fed by the troubles of our times, not just the reality of those troubles but exaggerated misrepresentations of them by significant persons in Susan's life.

"For all who are in this room, let me trace the story of a frightened little girl, let's say a ten-year-old seeing the best of her world through the eyes of an angry, disappointed, belligerent, prejudiced father. A father who cursed and condemned, and shouted and seethed and divided the world into good and evil. His world was a world of righteousness and order and duty, a religious world, the world of a God who was kind and merciful. The other world he described and feared was one of wickedness, conquest, destruction, a world of evil, a world of Satan and damnation and Communism.

"Susan was an only child and somewhat withdrawn from outsiders.

114

Her father appeared strong and wise and kind and good. Olaf Larson loved Susan and enjoyed her presence. Like many parents he gave no thought to the effect his words might have on his young daughter. In fact, he took pleasure in appearing strong and righteous as he won her admiration. He knew his words impressed her and in his mind he believed these were things she needed to know and be keenly aware of. (But I ask you, at age ten?)

"Susan not only heard his words; they left their indelible mark in her mind. In their transfer from his lips to her mind, she absorbed the kindred feelings; and fear darkened her life and shadowed her days. Her youthful mind wove its own web of danger and evil, and spread tentacles of malevolence to people she didn't know and distrust toward people she did know. Then one day, Sister Barbara whom you met yesterday, reached out to her with concern and kindness. Her words cleared the road ahead, but only temporarily, when she said with conviction to Susan, "You're one of God's children."

"But the battle wasn't won. About the time Susan was finishing Saint Edward's High School, her father ran for mayor of Seattle. His battle with the Communists became increasingly personal as the Communist party grew, infiltrated the unions, and entered the fray to defeat her father whom they called 'lying Larson.' The evil world once more knocked loudly and persistently at the Larson door and their home became a verbal battleground where Olaf's curses and accusations damned the Communists to hell. As their leaders and sympathizers continued attacking Olaf verbally, he translated their behavior as physically dangerous 'to all of us'. Susan described for me family scenes during this time. Her father used to actually shout curses and pound his fists when anyone questioned Senator McCarthy's search for Communists in our Congress, in the FBI, in Hollywood, really everywhere.

"To add fuel to the fire inside Susan, there came the weekly talks by Bishop Sheen who vehemently condemned Communism as the work of the devil. When the news media suggested that Bishop Sheen had accurately predicted the death of Stalin, she felt increasingly vulnerable to a personal attack by the Communists who, in her mind, were becoming progressively more violent and dangerous after Stalin's death. The outcome became clearer in her muddled thinking: murder of her parents and herself was imminent.

"As terror turned full blast on Susan, she was nearing graduation from high school. As you heard from prior testimony and saw from the exhibit of her school record, she abruptly came to a point where she could hardly function and was looking to withdraw from life. Susan's parents began attending Mass during the week and Susan joined them praying for safety and to avoid the imminent danger. Then she decided to go to Seattle College, motivated partly by seeing it as a refuge from evil. The planning offered her a temporary respite but it did nothing to halt the paranoid process now well ensconced in her mind.

"You heard Mr. Hanson's testimony about why Susan did not want children and how she maneuvered to avoid getting pregnant. By this time in her life, this nest of evil was contemporary. It didn't increase and lessen. It didn't come and go. It was there, perhaps fluctuating between 'active' or 'inactive', but there constantly. Let me remind you of a few occasions when it was active. These are all based on the testimony you heard yesterday.

"Edith Tracey testified as to the strange behavior of Susan the night they wanted to watch the Bishop Sheen program on TV. I learned from Susan the reason she left the room. She believed the Merks had joined the communists. They wanted to see Susan's reaction to Sheen's talk. If she was enthusiastic about Sheen, the Merks would report it to the communists and they would find her and kill her. One might say, 'An unreasonable thought.' I would say, 'You're right!' But reason was not functioning adequately for Susan.

"You've heard two people who worked with Susan testify. One was her supervisor. There was nothing untoward about her behavior at work. When I questioned Susan about leaving her job, she told me two of the women in the office were active communists. Susan told me the two used to stand at the water fountain and talk about her; and when they passed her desk they tried to see what she was working on. She believed there were others in the office who were communists, but she **knew** those two women were.

"We end this sad story by returning to the beginning of my testimony, the day I went to see Susan in the Seattle jail. That day I sat on the bench in her cell for twenty minutes or more, trying to persuade her at least to talk to me. I finally decided I was not going to be successful so I told Susan I was leaving and doubted I would have the judge's permission to return. I called the officer to unlock the cell door so I could go. He unlocked it and as he opened it, Susan made a throated sound, not really a word I could distinguish. As I turned toward Susan she was looking at me. I returned to the bench.

Slowly, carefully, guardedly she told the story. You've heard testimony from Susan's husband and from the victim's husband, each suggesting there was something amiss the evening before Lucille Blair died. And indeed there was. When the two couples were out for dinner, Lucille went to the bathroom and stopped briefly to speak to a couple of people at one of the tables. In Susan's mind Lucille was exchanging information with the "two communists" sitting there. That simple act set off alarm bells in Susan's haunted hidden inner nest of fear and danger. When they got in the car Susan sat with Lucille because she **needed to keep an eye on her**, as she said. And after she got home she raised the question twice with her husband: **why did Lucille stop to talk to those two people.** He passed if off as insignificant. **But it was not insignificant to Susan.**

Susan had a restless night and by the time she arose that fate-filled Sunday morning, she believed the Communists were near-by and planning to kill her. I did not take notes during my interview with Susan. Doing so would have blocked her willingness to talk to me. But I wrote down our exchange of words as soon as I left the jail. These are her words as I remembered them: 'When I came to the living room Sunday morning I went to look out the front window because I was anxious to know what the Blair's were doing. When I pulled up the shade I saw Lucille come out on her porch and pick up the Sunday paper. As she picked up the paper she looked up the street toward the intersection. The way she picked up the paper and looked up the street was a signal to the Communists waiting at the corner. **It was time for me to be killed.**"

Susan reacted to defend herself. She had often fantasized a communist attack. How it might come? How she might defend herself? In these fantasies she always defended herself. The world would be better off if she could kill even one or two of them. Her father would be proud. Susan went to the kitchen, picked up a butcher knife, walked across the street, rang the doorbell and when Lucille opened the door Susan stabbed her to save herself from imminent death by the Communists.

"Susan spent this last year at the Braceland Institute. Our further evaluation has confirmed what I suspected after my first interview. Susan is diagnosed as having *Paranoid Schizophrenia*. During this past year of therapy and medication she has regained an ability to distinguish between what she knows to be true and what she used to believe to be true, particularly in regard to Communism which was the focus and substance of her delusional thinking. Therapy has assisted her in acknowledging the exaggerated responses of her father to a realistic but limited battle with the communist influence of those years. She has come to realize that her attachment to her father was an important factor in misleading her as well as her mother in their attitudes and beliefs.

"That is the story of Susan Hanson as we have come to know it at the Institute."

Mr. Craven: "Thank you Dr. Moke for helping us understand this sad and tragic story. Let me ask you a couple of questions. Do you believe Susan Hanson knew what she was doing when she stabbed Lucille Blair?"

Doctor Moke: "Yes, I believe she knew what she was doing."

Mr. Craven: "And did Susan Hanson intend to kill Lucille Blair?"

Doctor Moke: "Yes, I believe she intended to kill Lucille Blair?

Mr. Craven: "And was Susan Hanson in control of her reasoning, of her mental capacity at that time?"

Doctor Moke: "No, I believe she was not in control of her reasoning or mental capacity at that time. She suffered from long standing paranoid delusions and was defending herself from someone whom she believed to be intent on causing her death. She acted in self-defense toward someone whom she saw as an unjust aggressor."

Mr. Craven: "Thank you for your testimony. I reserve the right to recall this witness."

After a "No Cross" from Gloria Wilson, Judge Craven asked, "Are there other witnesses for the defense?"

Mr. Craven: "I call Doctor Ralph Rogers to the stand." After the swearing in, Mr. Craven continued: "Please state your name, your credentials and your relationship to the defendant."

Doctor Rogers: "My name is Ralph Rogers, I'm a Board Certified Psychiatrist, I'm a member of the medical staff at Braceland Institute, and I have been Susan Hanson's primary therapist during her hospitalization at the Institute."

Mr. Craven: "You have heard Doctor Moke's testimony. Would you agree or disagree with any of Doctor Moke's statements and particularly his answers regarding diagnosis and mental capacity?"

Doctor Rogers: "I would agree with his testimony including his statements regarding diagnosis and mental capacity."

Mr. Craven: "If Susan Hanson were to be found not guilty by this jury, would you have any recommendations to make to the Court in regard to her release?"

Doctor Rogers: "Whatever the results of the jury deliberations, I would recommend Ms. Hanson be returned to Braceland Institute after the trial for further assessment to evaluate what effect this ordeal may have had on her emotional state. If she is found innocent, I would still recommend the assessment and a favorable report provided to the court before she is finally released. Recommendations for suitable follow-up care should also be prescribed in that report."

Mr. Craven: "Thank you for your testimony Doctor Rogers. Your honor, the defense has nothing further."

After "No cross" from Gloria Wilson, Judge Charles gave instructions to the jury and dismissed them. Court was adjourned. It was eleven a.m.

Craven, Rogers and Moke went to lunch together and wandered back to the court about one thirty in the afternoon. It was an hour later when word came that the jury had reached a verdict.

The court convened and went through a brief and orderly process. The unanimous jury decision was "Not Guilty." The judge accepted the verdict and ordered Susan Hanson to return to Braceland Institute pending a thorough evaluation and report to the court when Ms. Hanson was ready to be discharged. That report was to be signed by two Institute psychiatrists.

Of course, the defense team was delighted with the unanimous verdict. Susan Hanson was brought back to the hospital that afternoon. When Doctor Moke saw her later that evening, Susan said, "You have brought me from a dark dungeon in my mind and in my life. I will always be grateful for your care and the care of Dr. Rogers and all who have worked with me here."

Doctor Moke replied, "Susan, you brought yourself from that dungeon you speak of. We gave you a hand up, but you opened yourself to others and you pieced together the parts we helped you examine from a fresh, independent, adult perspective. Your father and mother were good honest people reacting to the stress and harshness of their own lives. And there was certainly plenty of it, especially for your father. They were completely unaware of how impressionable their daughter was. Your father vented his anger with words but his behavior was never really inappropriate. He was in fact a good Christian man. Remember that as you move on in life; and you will move on.

"We'll see how things go for you for a short time; and before long I think you will be back with your husband. In fact, after the first few days, it might be a good idea for you occasionally to spend a few hours off grounds with Oscar. The two of you will have lots to talk about and undoubtedly would appreciate some privacy."

Things went well for Susan. She was sleeping well, eating well and participating in a variety of programs available for the non-acute patient population. Her anti-psychotic medicine was decreased with continuing emotional stability. After the first week passed Doctor Rogers recommended she have the off-ground passes Moke had mentioned to her. After a couple of short passes, they were extended to six hours, later to eight and by the end of six weeks Doctor Rogers talked with Doctor Moke and they agreed overnight passes could begin.

During these off-grounds passes Susan and Oscar spent time looking for another house and they eventually found a cozy two-bedroom with a nice mountain view.

Three months after Susan's trial and return to Braceland Institute Judge Charles received the following letter:

Dear Judge Charles,

Susan Hanson returned to Braceland Institute on April 6, 1967 following her trial for the murder of Lucille Blair, at which she was found innocent. You ordered that she be returned to Braceland Institute for further evaluation with the provision that when she was deemed ready for discharge the hospital would notify you based on the decision and signature of two Institute psychiatrists.

At this time the undersigned state that as of this date Susan Hanson is considered of healthy mind and able to function outside of a hospital setting. Arrangements have been made for follow-up care with Doctor Benjamin Storch, a reputable psychiatrist in Tacoma.

Respectfully submitted,
Ralph Rogers, M. D. Stephen Moke, M.D.

On receipt of the letter, Judge Charles sent a brief note simply stating their letter had been received and he approved Mrs. Hanson's release.

The Institute staff had a quiet celebration with Mr. and Mrs. Hanson on the day of her discharge. It was not the usual pattern when a patient was discharged but the entire staff wanted something special for the occasion. Doctors Roger and Moke were in attendance and all said their farewells to the Hanson's.

On March fourth of the following year, Doctor Moke received a card announcing that Susan and Oscar were celebrating the birth of a six pound, four-ounce boy who would be named Stephen, in honor of the man who listened.

THE WOMAN WHO STOOD TALL

JALEE WAS IN A HURRY. SHE WORRIED SHE WOULDN'T GET BACK IN TIME to finish preparing lunch. While making soup that morning, she discovered she had no basil. Of course she could have skipped the basil but that was not the way Jalee did things. Her soup was well known to the town workmen, 'regulars' for lunch at the Jalee Café, the only café in the small community of Elm. Their lunch-time was limited. Her goal was always to meet their schedules.

So her only choice was to drive the eight miles to Gene's Groceries in the outskirts of Spokane, get the basil and hurry back. Gene's was popular with the Elm residents and people living in the Spokane suburb where it was located. Prices were reasonable and Jalee was a wise shopper for her café. The store was crowded as it always was on a Friday morning. As a regular customer Jalee went directly to the spices and picked up the small bottle of basil.

She walked rapidly to the check-out stations. There were four of them but only two were open. The lines were long. Jalee was well known to the manager and most of the employees. As she approached the nearest check-out station she held up the bottle to show the cashier and indicated she was in a hurry. This sort of thing had happened before and on one occasion she mentioned it to the store manager. His response was, "You're a regular, Jalee, and we all know you well. If you have one or two items and the lines are long just wave the items to show the cashier and pay the next time you come in. No one here would question your honesty. You're a regular customer; we know about your café in Elm and how vital it is to the people there. If you're in a hurry don't let our inefficiency slow you down."

Without a thought she left the store with the bottle of basil in her hand. A policeman stopped her as she walked away and asked to see her receipt. She briefly explained what happened and her personal arrangement with the store manager. The policeman would have none of it and without further conversation or inquiry asked to see her driver's license. Then he wrote her a summons for shoplifting. For a brief moment a shadow darkened her mind with the thought, "Is this a matter of racial prejudice or just a rookie policeman trying to make his mark?" She didn't have time for a lengthy explanation and intuition told her "talk" would be no value. She put the ticket in her pocket and was off to address the need of her soup.

The Jalee Café was open from eleven-thirty a.m. until three-thirty p.m. It served soup of the day, sandwiches (hot and cold), and two varieties of Jalee's home-made pies. Between twenty and thirty tradesmen, a dozen or more town merchants and residents and occasional visitors came to Jalee's Monday through Saturday; open on Saturdays because many of the tradesmen worked six day weeks. She considered them her primary customers and consequently catered to their needs.

Jalee's quiet kindness was known in the area. There were two or three old-timers living in Elm whom most considered as human fixtures in the town. They found different places to bunk depending on the weather and apparently found some of their food in garbage cans or hand-outs. A small church in town was known to them as a favorable food source. Rather regularly one or two or even the three of them would show up near the Jalee Café right around eleven-thirty. When Jalee spotted them outside (which was their expectation) she would invite them in with some comment, such as "I need someone to test the soup today and tell me if it's too spicy or too watery." Her invitations varied but their acceptance was standard. They were served a large bowl of soup and "here's a sandwich to go with the soup and help you make a better decision about it."

When Jalee got back to Elm she took up where she left off and finished lunch preparations. One of the old-timers showed up and after a test agreed with Jalee's opinion that the added basil was necessary. Lunch went well for the thirty-four cash-paying customers that day. She closed at three-thirty and after cleaning up thoroughly (as always), she put on her jacket to leave for home. She found the policeman's summons in her jacket pocket. During business hours she totally forgot the outside world. Serving her customers filled those hours. With the reminder in hand she decided, "I must remember to tell John about this."

John Clark worked in Spokane as Station Manager for the Northern Pacific Railroad. He had worked there for the past thirty years. Jalee could expect him home almost exactly at six-fifteen. He kept his personal schedule more accurate than most train schedules are. This particular March evening he was greeted by Jalee with the usual peck on the cheek and in her hand a summons ordering her to appear in municipal court within the next fifteen days or face arrest. The charge was theft and if found guilty the person could be sentenced to jail three to thirty days depending on the seriousness of the offence.

Dinner was delayed for twenty minutes while Jalee tried to explain what occurred at Gene's Groceries. Then they had dinner trying to avoid the topic that suddenly darkened their life. Increasing anxiety came with the dessert since they knew something would have to be decided. John was quite concerned. He knew how inwardly troubled Jalee could become over little things involving others. She had never told him details about the prejudice she experienced in earlier years but he observed her tension rise in the mildest confrontation with others, particularly if they were Caucasian, and most were. They had been man and wife for eighteen years. He felt there was much about Jalee he didn't know, not that she was secretive, but there was a privacy, a shield-like barrier that automatically blocked out certain areas of Jalee's past life.

Jalee typically worked out any problems at the café on her own. In fact, John never went to the café. Jalee ran it, did the shopping, the cleaning-up, the maintenance, the book-keeping and the taxes. She managed the business with competence and, one might say, with fervor.

Her anxiety and subsequent helplessness to respond to the policeman's ticket was not a surprise to John. Jalee was extremely competent in all things relating to the café, but interactions with strangers over ill-defined issues could be overwhelming for her. His various comments now were made to reassure her, although he wasn't sure himself how to approach the matter. He feared Jalee's appearance in court would be extremely unsettling and the damage to her self-respect could be disastrous. She would be concerned about town gossip. If a court hearing occurred, he knew it would weigh so heavily on Jalee she might want to close the café and keep to herself, perhaps even ask him to move to another area or even another town. John knew they couldn't go through a court appearance and the possibility of jail-time was unthinkable.

He decided he would call his personal physician, Doctor Mansfield, and ask his advice. Mansfield had been his internist for twenty years and John had complete confidence in him and his wisdom. When John told Jalee his plan, she appeared mildly reassured. Mansfield was also her physician.

The following Monday John took a break at work and called Doctor Mansfield. When Mansfield was on the phone, John explained the situation as briefly and as thoroughly as possible. When he finished, Mansfield said, "At the moment I don't know what to tell you, but I completely agree any kind of court appearance could be very detrimental to Jalee. Let me talk to my partner and get back to you. He's had some experience with a new doctor in our building, a psychiatrist. Could I call you this evening at home?" John said he'd welcome the evening call.

It was about seven-thirty that evening when Doctor Mansfield called. After a brief exchange about the wild rain and lightning storm of the day, Mansfield said, "I've talked with my colleague, Dr. Brenner. He told me his wife has been seeing Doctor Stephen Moke for the last six months or so. Moke is the psychiatrist I mentioned to you earlier. He moved into our building ten months ago. Brenner's wife, Joyce, spoke very highly of Doctor Moke and heartily recommended him. I also gave Brenner some idea of what you are dealing with, not revealing any names. After a lengthy discussion we finally agreed it **could possibly** be beneficial if you took Jalee to see Doctor Moke. I'm not sure what he could do but he might come up with something. This in no way suggests Jalee has a mental illness; if you decide to do this you should make that crystal clear to her. Since Jalee is also my patient I'm aware of her sensitivity in interpersonal matters. By the way, it is helpful I have a signed consent from both you and Jalee to discuss your care with each other. I have to say this is the only idea Brenner and I could come up with."

Jalee was finished with the dishes by the time John was off the phone. They sat on the sofa to discuss Doctor Mansfield's recommendation or perhaps "proposal" was more accurate. John chose his words carefully because he knew it was a delicate matter for Jalee and above all he didn't want his statements to disturb her further. He finally got to the kernel. "After talking with Doctor Mansfield and considering there are few possibilities, in fact we couldn't think of one other than this one, we agreed it would be worth a try. There is a new psychiatrist in Mansfield's building who comes highly recommended. When I mention psychiatrist, I absolutely and in no way mean to suggest you have a mental illness. Doctor Mansfield and I agreed that a psychiatrist can often see situations from a different perspective and discover factors that anyone else wouldn't have considered. I think it's worth a try, Jalee. Do you want to think it over for a day or two? Of course we don't have a lot of time and it might be difficult to get an appointment with this Doctor Moke."

The first part of Jalee's reply was not unusual. She was interested in names and always wondered about a person's place of origin. "I wonder where this Moke got that name and what country his family came from. I'd guess his ancestry is probably Scandinavian. But as for seeing him, it gets down to a question of which shame to choose: going to a psychiatrist or going to court. I guess I'll choose seeing the psychiatrist. I assume it will be a private meeting, just me, no one else." John was not surprised about the privacy statement. It was the core of her existence.

The following day John called Doctor Moke's office and after a long wait got through to him. "I'm John Clark and I'm calling to get an appointment for my wife, Jalee. Doctor Mansfield referred us to you and he will give you some background information about Jalee if you are able to give her an appointment. We need the appointment within the next week. There is a court situation pending and time is limited. We're feeling rather desperate."

Doctor Moke checked his office schedule. There were no openings. But there was something appealing in this man's voice, a pleading tone on behalf of his wife. He hated to turn them down. Normally his day ended at five; but after further thought he decided a five o'clock appointment wouldn't ruin his life. He'd be finished by six-thirty. "I can see your wife on Thursday of this week at five p.m. The interview will last approximately to six-thirty. Will that work for you and your wife?"

John responded, "That will be great. Thank you so much for making it possible. I'll let Doctor Mansfield know and I'm sure he'll be in touch with you. We'll be at your office this Thursday well before five."

It was with relief John hung up the phone, only to pick it up again and call Mansfield's office. He gave the secretary the information with a reminder for Mansfield to call Doctor Moke.

Doctor Mansfield called Doctor Moke later that afternoon. He introduced himself, "I'm Doctor Mansfield in an office two floors above you. I'm an internist. I know you're relatively new in the Lidger Building. I've heard some positive comments about you from colleagues. John Clark

126

tells me you have given his wife an appointment later this week. They are both patients of mine.

"If you have a couple of minutes I'd like to tell you a little about Jalee, John's wife. She owns and manages a small café in Elm. She is in general good health. Jalee is a Native American who through the years experienced the prejudice that was shamefully familiar to us all when we played cowboy and Indian games as children. There was some tragedy in her early days undoubtedly exacerbated by the unfortunate common use of the word 'redskin' for Native Americans. She is extremely sensitive about her heritage and at the same time remarkably proud of it. She is currently charged with theft and is in danger of being sent to jail. Her husband appealed to me for help. My partner and I discussed the situation and finally agreed a psychiatrist might find some basis to ward off the degradation jail-time would be for her. I hope you can find some way to help her, Doctor Moke."

Moke replied, "Your call has been helpful and thanks for the referral. I will certainly do my best to make her comfortable during our interview and elicit enough information to make a case on her behalf. I hope I get to meet you someday, Doctor Mansfield. Thanks for the information."

Thursday evening came and John and Jalee Clark were in Doctor Moke's waiting room well before five. Doctor Moke stepped out of his office promptly at five and introduced himself. "I'm Doctor Stephen Moke and I'm pleased to meet you both. Mrs. Clark, would you be comfortable coming into my office by yourself? I would prefer to interview you alone. Your husband can either wait here or return at six-thirty when our interview should be over. I want you both to know at this time that all conversations between Mrs. Clark and me will be completely confidential and I will not discuss them with anyone without Mrs. Clark's expressed permission." Jalee spoke to John briefly and then stood to accompany Doctor Moke.

In the office Doctor Moke motioned to a chair for Jalee and then he walked around a large, low coffee table to a chair on the other side. As always he made mental notes of a patient's initial appearance and demeanor. The observation often gave him a hint of what was to come. Jalee was noticeably erect as she walked and as she sat. He judged her height to be about five feet ten inches, but she looked taller because of her bearing. High forehead, prominent cheek bones, straight nose, slightly darker skin, black hair. He probably wouldn't have noticed she was Native American if he passed her on the street, but "the appearance" would be noticeable to those for whom it would "make a difference."

Doctor Moke had received a phone call from her husband earlier in the day and knew the story of the policeman giving Jalee a summons. He began the interview. "Mrs. Clark, do you mind if I call you Jalee?" She nodded and he continued. "I spoke with Doctor Mansfield and with your husband about the situation we are here to discuss. I will now review what I have been told. If anything is inaccurate, please, interrupt me and let me know."

Doctor Moke briefly reviewed the information about her trip to the grocery store and the events surrounding the charge of theft and her expected court appearance. Jalee maintained her straight posture and continued to nod her assent as Moke covered what he had been told. Then he moved to personal questions searching for information that would give him at least some basic understanding of Jalee's background and her view of the legal issues she was facing. Up to this point she had maintained a response pattern of nods or a quiet "yes."

Now Moke's questions required Jalee's answers which came thoughtfully and quietly without show of emotion. As her story came out, Doctor Moke noted her resigned manner and the monotone of her words. His years of experience enabled him to watch subtle facial expressions which often occur unconsciously as someone recalls information from the past. As he watched Jalee his thoughts were, "There are powerful emotions at play in this woman's life, but they are locked away by the shelter of time and distance and a busy life which keep them somewhat blurred, but not buried. They are probably easily aroused in the presence of a Caucasian man or woman."

In response to his careful and discerning questions he obtained important information about Jalee's history. She and her brother, five years older, were the children of two Native Americans. She announced with pride, "We are of the Spokane Tribe of the Salish Family. The Spokanes are Children of the Sun." Her father died of tuberculosis when they lived in Omak on the Colville Reservation. Jalee was nearing four when he died. She commented in a matter-of-fact way, "Father still speaks with me."

Less than two years after her father's death, her mother and the two children left the reservation to live with her maternal grandfather on a small piece of land a few miles east of Spokane. Several Native Americans lived on small patches in the same area. They eked a meager living from their gardens, raising a few goats, chickens, or other productive animals and fishing in the Spokane River.

They hadn't been there but a few months when Jalee was walking home from Spokane with her mother and brother on a summer evening. Her mother and brother were on the right edge of the highway going east toward Coeur d'Alene. Jalee was walking in the grass along the side of the road "looking for pretty stones." Abruptly the blast of a honking horn got her attention. She looked up just in time to see a car slam into her mother and brother knocking them off the road. She spoke slowly, deliberately, word following word as she looked into Moke's eyes, "There—were—two—white—men—in the front seat. —They were—laughing. They didn't stop! They didn't stop!" Her jaw was clinched. Her eyes were wet. She sat even taller.

With his own watery eyes Doctor Moke knew she would not cry. It was pride in her heritage, a stoic response to a hostile world, awareness of the Great Spirit who was the foundation stone of her life. Moke let the silence embrace them both and in the silence he *knew the rest*. Her mother and brother were with the Great Spirit and Jalee was alone. Alone with her maternal grandfather, whom Moke later learned was not the best of caregivers, not the kindest of men.

The police came and called an ambulance to take the bodies. They asked Jalee what happened. She told them just as she told Moke. They offered Jalee a ride home which she refused. As far as she knew there was never any further investigation of the accident (Jalee said "of the murder"). With a dismissive shrug of her shoulders she said, "They were just a couple of 'redskins'." Jalee was five at the time.

By the coming September Jalee was six. She wanted to go to school but her grandfather was opposed to it. He called her "stupid and foolish" for wanting an education. He said, "Why would someone like you want an education? What could you do with it? It won't get you anywhere in the *white man's world*." He constantly belittled her and blamed her for the death of her mother and brother. He said she should have been watching for cars instead of "playing in the grass. You're always playing. You don't care about anyone else. That's not our way. We watch out for each other. It's our belief, our heritage. We need always to stand together. You failed in your duty."

Even at her early age Jalee knew her grandfather was failing in his duty to her. Regarding school Jalee defied her grandfather and walked with three of the neighbor children to attend the nearest public grade school three miles away. The four of them bore the daily taunts and cruelty of their classmates through the years. "Wigwam warriors, redskin robbers, brave bitches" were a few of the many names they were called on the playground and in the classroom. When they walked to school, as they passed even some of the adults would say, "Why don't you go back to the reservation where you belong?"

Doctor Moke asked, "How did you respond to all this?"

Jalee calmly answered, "I didn't respond. I made a shell, a wikiup in my mind and I'd go there not to hide but to talk to my father or to commune with the Great Spirit. But I never became hardened to the abuse or by the abuse."

Jalee moved on with her life story. "In those days there was a high school for Native Americans on the Colville Reservation. If I was determined to continue my education my grandfather wanted me to go there. Instead I went to the public high school in Spokane. I rode my bicycle or walked the five miles on snowy days. In high school a few of my classmates were more sociable toward me but rarely came to my defense when others made fun of me."

She stopped, waiting for Moke's questions to direct her. He did with, "And what happened after you finished high school?"

"When I was seventeen (and still in school) I began working in the restaurant at the Davenport Hotel. I worked two evenings a week and on weekends. When I was there I talked so seldom some of the people thought I was mute. I watched and listened and I learned. I decided someday I wanted to have a restaurant so I could share in feeding others. It seemed a good thing to do and I believed my father would be proud of me for doing it. When we lived on the reservation, some people were starving and no one could help them. My father told stories of hunger and starvation in the history of our Salish people. He told me the story of *The Trail of Tears*, a story every Native American was familiar with in those days.

"I couldn't wait to leave my grandfather's house and I did so the day I turned eighteen. He treated me as his servant after my mother and brother were killed. He had no interest in my life and reached a point where he rarely spoke to me other than to make a demand or issue a command."

Jalee seemed startled by all she said. She had let her guard down momentarily. "It's a good sign; she can cross the barrier she has erected in her mind," Moke thought. Then he said, "Tell me a little about your current life. How are things at home? Do you enjoy the café and the work involved?"

Jalee seemed quite willing to move on to pleasanter times. "John and I have been married eighteen years. We have no children. John is good to me.

I collect stray dogs and feed them scraps from the café, not left-overs from customer's plates but food I didn't get to serve. John doesn't particularly like having stray dogs around; but he's good about it and doesn't complain. We live our separate lives but have a sense of companionship that is supportive and comfortable."

In a brighter tone she continued, "I love the café and treat my regular customers as friends. They are friends! I make no judgments about anyone who comes in. There are no distinctions of color, of sex, of religion, or of manners or of dress and certainly not of ancestry. No one is ever rowdy or inappropriate. If a newcomer talks a little off-color or gets out-of-line in any way, a 'regular' will speak quietly to the person about it. As I think about it now, I could say it's a calm, comfortable, peaceful place open to serve anyone and everyone."

Doctor Moke was thinking, "What a remarkable woman! She has borne the bitterness of racial abuse throughout her life. In return, by her presence, her demeanor, and (he couldn't help but think) by her stature she has brought a normally noisy and sometimes coarse group of working men to a quiet, peaceful lunch-time setting." He moved on to other things, "How do spend your free time? What do you enjoy doing when you're not working?"

Jalee was quick to respond, "I read books, all kinds of books. I read and read: histories, biographies, the classics, poetry. I love poetry. The *Sonnets from the Portuguese* are so beautiful I memorized some of them. I read through the quiet times of day. I spend hours outside taking care of the dogs and just watching the sky, the clouds, the twilight, the stars: a whole world with wonderful messages and meanings even more beautiful than *Sonnets from the Portuguese*." Moke had the impression Jalee was on the border of that other world even as she spoke.

Doctor Moke decided it was about time to end the interview; not because of the time itself but because he decided he had gained enough from their conversation to write a letter to the court on Jalee's behalf. He was reluctant to stop because he felt there was much more about Jalee's life that would be interesting to know. But she didn't come to be his patient; she came for an evaluation and that was finished. However, partly because of his professional interest, but mostly to strengthen her position with the court he decided to recommend she see him again every two weeks for three visits. He thought, "Judges tend to be more lenient when someone else is participating in the burden of their decision."

He explained to Jalee, "It's about time to end our conversation. Let me explain my plan to you. I will ask your husband to give me the judge's name and I will compose a letter to the judge this evening. It will be hand-delivered to the court tomorrow morning. It is my hope you will receive a reply from the court within the next day or two; and it is also my hope the judge will be lenient. There is one thing I want to make clear. In the letter I will tell the court that I will continue to see you in my office for three visits over the next six weeks. I will note this recommendation is not based on any evidence of mental illness. I will tell the judge this experience has been seriously unsettling for you and the additional visits will be for the purpose of assuring me that you have no lasting mental or emotional disruption as a result of the summons. Is what I've just said understandable and acceptable? Any need for clarification?"

Jalee responded, "It all sounds fine and is acceptable to me. Then I should make another appointment for two weeks from now?" They discussed a possible time and Moke gave her an appointment at four p.m. on the same day two weeks later.

Doctor Moke escorted her to the waiting room. John was there and in response to Moke's question said Judge George Biller was the sitting judge on the municipal court for the month. John asked about the bill and paid for the session in cash. Moke told him Jalee would be coming for an additional three visits and the reason he was recommending them. He told John what the fee would be for the additional regular visits, adding it could be paid at visit time or be billed the end of the month.

After dinner that evening Stephen Moke typed a letter to Judge Biller on office letterhead:

Dear Judge Biller,

This letter is written on behalf of Jalee Clark, wife of John Clark who is Station Manager at the Northern Pacific Railroad. She is scheduled to appear in your court within the next three days. About three weeks ago she was issued a summons for theft at Gene's Groceries in Spokane.

Jalee owns and manages a small café in Elm. She is respected by the people of her community and admired for her generosity to the poor. Her café is frequented for lunch by the tradesmen and laborers of the area. She works alone in the café. One morning she was missing a spice for the luncheon soup so she hurried to Gene's Groceries to get it. Check-out lines were long. She waved the jar of spice for a clerk to see and walked out of the store. She had an arrangement with the manager to do this if she were in a hurry as she was that day. She would routinely pay the store on her next return. A policeman saw what she did and as she exited the store he wrote out the summons which is now before you. Mrs. Clark tried to explain to the officer the understanding she had with the store management but the officer apparently would not listen to her.

At the request of her internist, I did a psychiatric assessment of Mrs. Jalee Clark this afternoon with the purpose of addressing the issue of the summons and the events related to it. I have found no evidence of psychiatric illness but on the basis of my interview I found the danger of a grave injustice possibly occurring. Jalee Clark is a full-blooded Native American of the Spokane tribe. She experienced severe racial prejudice throughout her early life. When she was five years old, she witnessed her mother and ten-year-old brother killed by two Caucasian males in a hit and run accident. Apparently the incident was never thoroughly investigated. Through grade and high school, she continued to suffer from the harshness of the racism which unfortunately continues to permeate our local culture.

Jalee Clark is caring to her neighbors, kind to her customers, generous to the needy. She lives by the Native American creed of respect for all the Great Spirit's creatures, human and other. She cares for wandering animals primarily stray dogs.

Mrs. Clark has agreed to return to my office to talk with me every two weeks over the next six weeks. I have asked her to do so because this whole episode has been most unsettling for her. I feel a professional responsibility to monitor her well-being until this crisis in her otherwise stable and peaceful life has subsided.

In closing this letter, I will say, "Putting Mrs. Clark in jail for a day or even a minute might kill her, perhaps not physically but it would kill the proud Spokane-Salish spirit that enables her to treat others well in spite of their short-comings, their hostile behavior and the tragic events of her own life."

If you have any questions regarding this matter, please call me. My professional card is enclosed.

Sincerely,

Stephen Moke, M.D.

Ann Moke, Stephen's wife, served as his secretary, accountant, and errand person as needed. One might add to the list, as a retired social worker she was also Stephen's confidante and often reviewed his cases with him. She checked the letter and delivered it the next morning to the municipal court. That afternoon Judge Biller called John Clark at the Northern Pacific and informed him that on the basis of a letter received from Doctor Stephen Moke charges against Jalee Clark were summarily dismissed.

That evening Doctor Moke had a phone call from Doctor Mansfield reporting on the call he had from John Clark and the call John received from Judge Biller. Mansfield ended the call, "You did a great service to Jalee and John. And you've also done a service to the workmen and citizens of the Elm area. I understand the Jalee Café is very popular there. My partner and I are personally grateful for your willingness to intervene so promptly and so capably. It is good to know we have your expertise available in the Lidger Building."

Stephen shared the news with Ann as they enjoyed a Southern Comfort Manhattan in honor of Jalee Clark and to celebrate the outcome of a successful intervention in a worthy case.

It was two weeks later when Jalee was greeted by Doctor Moke as he opened the waiting room door at four p.m. on Thursday. She was alone and Doctor Moke assumed she came directly from the café. As they entered the office Jalee went directly to her chair. As Doctor Moke passed her he doubted she would offer her hand in gratitude and he was right. It would not be proper decorum for a Native American woman to offer her hand in any situation. Instead she spoke, "Thank you Doctor Moke for rescuing me two weeks ago. The court appearance alone would have been unbearable. I don't know how I could have survived the shame."

Doctor Moke replied, "It was your willingness to come to my office and talk with me as you did that made the letter a possibility. It was a privilege for me to be involved in preventing the policeman's behavior becoming a stain on your life and your reputation. Was there any gossip about it?"

Jalee responded, "I heard none and I do hear most of the town gossip in the café. Customers treat me as if I'm deaf. They talk about anything and everything as I move around the room. I hear about the family quarrels, the unhappy unions, the troubled teens, the difficult bosses; it's as if all the troubles in the world come to Jalee's café. I don't try to listen and I'd rather not hear them. I have my own difficulties. Hearing the difficulties of others doesn't make me feel any better."

It occurred to Moke, "Is Jalee identifying with my situation? Is she really wondering how I manage in my practice to deal with the problems of others all the time? Is she wondering if I can hear her thoughts and feelings and not be affected by them? I should check this out." So he said, "Do you ever confide some of your life story, significant events that have occurred, to anyone else? Perhaps to John or to a friend?" As Jalee shook her head rather strongly, Moke asked, "You seemed comfortable talking to me two weeks ago about some painful and difficult times in your life. Will you be able to continue talking to me about things that have happened or might happen in the future? And more importantly will you feel free to do so?"

Jalee didn't answer right away but was obviously considering his questions. Her reply was slow and deliberate. "I've been thinking about that since I was last here. When I talked to you two weeks ago it was certainly helpful. I don't mean just because of the letter you wrote. Talking seemed to bring greater clarity to my thinking, not just a clarity but a feeling of calm and a sense of peace. Most of what I told you had never been put into words. I was almost surprised that I found the words and was able to say them out loud to someone. I have no close friends or family to talk to; and John and I never talk about personal matters."

Doctor Moke replied, "Has there ever been anyone in your life in whom you did confide or even just talk to about things that were happening to you or ideas you had? Or just about your feelings?"

Jalee had a sort of winsome look as she said, "Oh, when I was little I talked to my father all the time. I told him how I slept, what I ate, what games I played, what I did with my brother, everything I could think of. He would hold me on his lap and listen to every word. He never got tired of listening to his 'Jalee chatterbox' as he used to call me. He died three weeks before my fourth birthday. I missed him terribly. His death was the worst thing that ever happened in my life. I was sad and often just sat and remembered him. I didn't want to talk to anyone else and I soon stopped talking. I felt like I couldn't talk any more. I said it all to my father. There was nothing more to say. He was gone. My mother began to worry about my silence. Then she became frightened because I stayed by myself and wouldn't talk to anyone for over a month after his death.

"Then one day I was sitting outside the house thinking of my father and suddenly a bird chirping in a nearby tree got my attention. The chirp sounded like '*Ja-lee, Ja-lee,*' the way my father said my name. It was almost like I'd been deaf and began to hear again. In my mind I answered. No, it wasn't just in my mind. I whispered, 'Father, I'm here and I can hear you.' I continued talking and we had the first of our secret conversations: me in the yard, father with the Great Spirit. We still talk when I call to him. I sometimes don't say the words out loud; when he answers he doesn't use words I hear but I *know* his response.

Moke sensed this was not an area to go farther into at this time. He wanted to get more history. He said, "You didn't tell me much about your life after you left your grandfather's house until the time you married John. I've been wondering how you came to open the café in Elm." It didn't take a direct question to prompt a response from Jalee.

Moke wondered if Jalee had been thinking about the past in anticipation of her visit and the kind of information he might ask about. Her responses seemed too well organized to be spontaneous. "When I left my grandfather's I moved to a one room apartment with kitchen privileges in Spokane, and I continued working at the Davenport. I met a young Caucasian man who worked as a busboy at the restaurant. I can't say 'I fell in love' but I found him attractive and enjoyed spending time with him. It occurs to me now, I was probably impressed because a Caucasian male treated me well. He crossed that imaginary line which in my experience existed between Caucasian and Native American. Or did I cross the boundary? Was I over-reaching my race? Was I foolishly flattered? I was extremely naïve then. The only prior experience with boys was their taunting, calling me names 'red robin _____' I won't say the other words they used. One boy always said, 'Let me nestle in your red robin nest?'" I didn't know anything about sex. It was never mentioned in my family. I knew enough to be curious before I was eighteen and on my own. Jim Wilson, the busboy, said he would teach me. His lesson turned into a pregnancy.

"Jim was soon called up in the draft. Before he left for Vietnam we were married by a Justice of the Peace. Some months later I saw my grandfather wandering around outside the Davenport, possibly looking for me. I confronted him and told him I was married, that my husband was in the infantry service and would soon leave for Vietnam. I also told him I was pregnant. Native Americans value family unity especially in times of need. He insisted I come live with him while I waited for the baby. He said the Great Spirit would be angry with him if he didn't provide food and shelter for his family during my pregnancy. Suddenly the world had become too big for me. I could take care of myself but my confidence did not extend to this child I was going to have. So I returned to live with my grandfather."

As Doctor Moke listened to Jalee, he noted how her features had softened, her voice had slowed, and her posture was more relaxed. He thought, "What a price individuals pay for the emotional baggage they carry through life? Native Americans apparently carried their tents and all their belongings as they moved from place to place. It was often a necessary that they leave behind no mark of their presence in an area. Jalee has carried her daily cares and emotional baggage silently, carefully, privately—and alone. Perhaps she shares things with her deceased father or the Great Spirit but the scars are still within her. And her journey will surely leave a mark and many will remember: *Jalee passed here.*

Jalee continued, "Six months after I moved in with my grandfather, I gave birth to my daughter, Susan. My grandfather was undoubtedly more proud than I was. By then Jim had shipped out to Vietnam. I wrote telling him the news. I never had a reply. Jim's unit returned to the States ten months later. But Jim's return was not to me. He filed for divorce and I signed the necessary papers. He never saw his daughter. My grandfather was furious when I told him what happened. He would have put me out of the house if it weren't for my daughter. After three months leave related to Susan's birth I returned to working at the Davenport.

"Grandfather (I always called him 'grandfather', his name was Joseph) took over the complete care of Susan soon after her birth. He got up at night when she cried; he gave her the bottles and fed her the baby food. He changed her, bathed her, played with her and rocked her. He wouldn't let me hold her, said I wasn't 'worthy'. If he fell asleep in the day or was out of the house for some reason, I'd hold her and talk to her. The lack of contact seemed to stifle my love for her. It probably sounds strange to you, but an attachment never developed between the two of us. Does that mean I'm an evil person, Doctor Moke?"

Moke thought it seemed such an innocent but significant question. He took some time preparing an appropriate answer, "No, Jalee, I don't think that means you are evil. You were prevented from caring for your daughter as mothers normally do. An infant *feels* the presence of their caregivers and those *feelings* bring comfort and relief from hunger, cold, wet diapers and other baby needs. At that same feeling level, a baby comes to recognize the voice, the manner, the touch of the caregiver. In this process the caregiver's feelings are aroused by the touching and feeding and bathing and rocking of the baby. You didn't have those opportunities. You were deprived of the caregiver's role. Those precious times are the foundation of a positive sense of self for the child and a lasting bond between child and caregiver. I assume your daughter and your grandfather retained a close bond."

Jalee replied, "Oh yes, Susan was always close to her great-grandfather and was devastated when he died some fifteen years ago. She barely spoke to me at his funeral which she arranged. I haven't seen her since."

Moke made a mental note. "Must talk someday about daughter Susan." Then he asked, "How did you ever manage to open the Jalee Café?" He was deliberately choosing a pleasanter subject for Jalee to talk about.

Jalee responded, "I lived off my tips for several years and saved my salary. I made notes about menus and portions, popular meals and less expensive meals, different dishes and how to prepare them and everything I could learn about the restaurant. One day I was serving the president of a local bank. He often requested seating at one of my tables. When I was serving his lunch he asked me what my plans were for the future. He remarked on my efficiency and pleasant manner. I told him I planned to have my own café someday. He suggested, if I was serious, I should stop at the bank some time and we could talk about a loan.

"About six months later I went to the bank to see him. By then I had scouted possible areas in and around Spokane. Elm was a small town with many small service suppliers for home owners. It was near a prominent Spokane residential area. I found a small building that seemed ideal for my plan. The bank president drove out with me one day and looked at it. He thought it was a good location and the building was a good buy. My savings met the bank's request for my percentage of the loan. I was in business!"

She said the words with pride and confidence and continued telling me all she did to get the café ready for service. She **had** chosen her location wisely and had assessed the need accurately. The Jalee Café thrived.

Doctor Moke said, "Our meeting time is up." Jalee appeared surprised and volunteered the comment that she would see him again in two weeks. He gave her the appointment card. After she left, Moke stepped into the waiting room. There was an envelope on the table. Inside was a check for the visit signed by Jalee. Money was never discussed. The check was always there after each session.

Jalee came to the session two weeks later. Doctor Moke immediately noted a more relaxed and outgoing manner. She was more spontaneous in choosing the things she wanted to talk about. Her favorite topic was the café and she also spoke about minor things that happened since her last visit.

At one point Jalee mentioned "my renters will be moving out this month." Doctor Moke questioned who the renters were and what did they rent. She responded, "Oh, I've never told you about my rental house. A few years after I opened the restaurant, a house three streets from the café came on the market. I looked at it and considered buying it. It was in poor condition and there was a lot of work to be done. I talked to John about it and he agreed it might be a good investment for me. I bought it with money from the café. I did much of the work getting it in condition to rent. I did the cleaning and painting and even replaced a couple of windows. I cleaned the yard, got some grass growing and got rid of all the trash. I paid a plumber and an electrician (café customers) to check it over and do whatever was necessary. My first renters were the young couple who are now leaving. They moved in about a week after I put the house up for rent. He's a teacher and will be going to teach in Yakima."

Doctor Moke commented, "That's remarkable, Jalee. I had no idea you were also a real estate investor. Do you think the house will be difficult to rent again?"

Jalee: "There's a good market for houses in Elm. It's a pleasant little community and a short drive to a number of businesses in Spokane. So when Bret and Penney leave I'll spruce it up and get it back on the rental market."

Much of the interview time was spent talking about the rental house and the community of Elm. Jalee said she is considering buying another house if a well-priced one comes on the market. It takes very little of her time to manage the property she has, and another "one or two would not over-load my schedule."

Doctor Moke was surprised at her entrepreneurship and asked, "Did you say 'one or two?'"

Jalee responded, "I plan to buy another house in the neighborhood of the café when one comes on the market. There's also a brick building in Elm that looks like a small church. It's been empty a long time. I don't know if it was built to be a church. I need to find out someday why it was originally built. If it was used as a church, I'd have to find out whether it would be appropriate to use it for another purpose."

Moke asked, "Where could you find out an answer to a question like that?"

Jalee made one of those responses that left Doctor Moke in a quizzical place, "There's *one I know who would let me know.*"

In a treatment session several months later Jalee reported that she bought the "old church building." It was built to be a church but was never occupied by the small congregation. A large portion of the money they collected to complete their final payment before occupancy was stolen by the parish treasurer who absconded. It was never used as a church. Jalee was already involved in modifying the space to convert the building to an unusual attractive rental house.

Doctor Moke was surprised when their time was over. He noticed Jalee moving forward in her chair before he checked the wall clock across the room. Jalee questioned, "I'll be here in two weeks at the same time? I don't really need an appointment card. Thank you for today." She stood and abruptly left the room.

On the day of her third and possibly last meeting, Moke was wondering how this would go. Would she request additional meetings? Or was she ready to say goodbye? Moke had no reason to suggest further sessions. The three meetings had provided an opportunity for her to talk about significant events in her life which she probably never spoke about to anyone. His sense was that Jalee found a certain relief in talking about family members, her marriage, her work history and her good fortune in finding a way to own and manage a place where laborers and merchants felt at home. The issue of court was never mentioned again once Jalee thanked him on her first return visit.

After they were seated Doctor Moke looked across the table for Jalee to begin. She was looking around the room in a careful manner, perhaps "a caring manner" was his thought. She seemed to "take in" each piece of furniture, each picture, even the lamps. She finally spoke, "This setting has become a comforting room for me. It often comes into my mind especially if I'm feeling weary or downhearted or troubled. I can see myself in this chair talking, putting my feelings into words. All the articles in the room encourage, what I've come to call, 'peace thoughts.' How did you choose everything? I would guess your wife was your decorator."

Moke was surprised by Jalee's remarks. They seemed quite personal, almost a bit invasive, especially the mention of his wife as decorator. He wondered: Is she indirectly trying to explore the possibility of additional visits? Is she hanging on to our relationship? Is there a racial boundary that prevents her asking for additional visits? Is the mention of his wife based on Native American propriety? He decided to respond to her directness with his own. "Your comments seem to suggest you might want to continue coming for visits and your question about my decorator surprises me. Yes, my wife was my decorator; but I wonder why you asked that?"

Jalee answered, "The room seems very home-like. It suggests contentment and peace. It's not austere and business-like as offices usually are, particularly doctor's offices. It seems to have a woman's caring touch. About another visit, yes, I would like to continue seeing you. I think my visits have made it easier for me to deal with those times when I feel anxious or irritable or sad. As I mentioned before, John and I don't talk much. By the end of the day, I sometimes feel gloomy and muddled. It's the time I usually go out and take care of the dogs. I tell them my troubles as they lick my hands and I pet them." Jalee smiled as the comparison became obvious. She added, "I don't mean to compare my visits here to the dogs licking my hands."

Moke smilingly responded, "Thank you for clarifying about the dogs. About visits, I will be available to see you as long as you wish. The frequency will be up to you. I'd suggest we continue every two weeks for now. If you want to change the frequency later on, just let me know." He was surprised at the insight Jalee had expressed. She recognized the emotions that were never expressed to others but were concealed so well behind her stand-offish, almost stoic demeanor; a pattern learned early in life and perhaps a racial characteristic.

Jalee looked relieved and moved into the usual pattern of their interviews: she would talk and Doctor Moke would comment or ask questions about the topic. "I'm getting something new for the café. I bought an old juke-box and I plan to put it in the café. I'll choose some old-time records and set it to play softly in the background during lunch hours. I don't want it to interfere with conversation but some days the men seem tired and talk very little except for a few comments about their work. I thought some music might brighten the time for them. I have a broad collection of classical music that is soothing and calming.

"Once I have it installed and it's in use for a few days I'll ask the regular customers whether or not they like it. I believe they'll give me their honest opinions. If they don't like it, I'll take it home but remember to play it only when John's not around." The last said with a smile.

Moke was surprised at Jalee's interest in and familiarity with music. He asked, "When did your interest in music begin? Was anyone in your family musical?"

Jalee replied thoughtfully, "My father played the flute. He played beautiful music, some of it was sad and then other tunes were happy ones. I would sit and watch him play. It seemed like the music came from his spirit and it always made me think of the Great Spirit. When I was in my teens I thought a lot about playing an instrument. Grandfather's flute was available because I kept it along with a few other things after he died. But I wouldn't play the flute; that was *his* and the *music was his.* I still have his flute tucked away in one of my special places at the house.

"When I left my grandfather's house and lived in a rented room, the family who lived there had a piano and let me use it. I learned to play the piano on my own (by ear I guess they call it). Before I married John I bought an old violin and learned to play just by trying. Next was a saxophone and after a couple of lessons I learned to play it. Since I married John I haven't played any instrument. He doesn't care for music. I sold my violin before we were married but I have the saxophone hidden away in a safe place at the café. I miss playing! I guess reading is a substitute but it's not as satisfying."

Doctor Moke wondered, "Do you think you'll ever play an instrument again? Or would you like to?"

Jalee was thoughtful. "I do miss it. Everything I do is so routine and regular, always the same. But music is creative; every note is like a spirit; it's born, it lives briefly, and it's gone. It leaves its breath in the world. It lives in our memory in a special way. Someday I'll play again!" The last words were a sort of declaration.

Jalee wore no watch but her sense of time was alert to the fact the session time was over. "It's about time for me to go. Can we continue our meetings every two weeks for the present? Is the same time available? It's a good time for me because I can finish everything at the café before I come here, and the time allows me to get home before John comes home. So I'm there to greet him."

Moke made a mental note, "Likes to be home to greet her husband but they talk very little." He replied, "This time is fine. I reserved it for you anticipating you might continue your visits. I hope these sessions will continue to be of value to you. Talking to someone does expand our view of life and the daily events that compose our immediate world. It's like taking a second look but through a different window. We'll meet again in two weeks, same time."

After the session was over and Moke reviewed it in his mind, he concluded that Jalee's father was the one person who gave her the precious gift of a positive self-awareness, her stature as a human, an individual, a special being. And that knowledge had naturally transferrd from her father to her relationship with the Great Spirit and back again to Jalee.

Jalee was Moke's last patient of the day. After she left he sat and thought about the session and wondered where Jalee's treatment would lead and what emotional change might occur. The sort of thing he did from time to time with his patients.

After dinner that evening he and Ann sat and chatted about their day. He spoke about Jalee and her story. He wondered how long he would be seeing her and how treatment would eventually come to a close. He appreciated talking over such thoughts with Ann and he regarded her as he would a supervisor. He valued not only her listening skills but the insights she brought to their discussions.

Ann responded to his comment, "I suspect you will be seeing Jalee for a long time. She is able to talk to you about the thoughts and feelings that have been part of her life and apparently remain meaningful. She has no other confidante and is not likely to develop one. It sounds like John is one of those men who live alone in their head as far as feelings go. They don't even acknowledge feelings to themselves much less ever reveal them to another. They are relatively immunized against the intrusion of feelings, their own or others.

"Jalee seems not to have any women friends and apparently never did. She is not likely to trust a Caucasian woman based on past interactions with them; and her business success and the physical stature you speak of might not be readily and culturally acceptable to a Native American woman. Her best bet is a Caucasian male who is willing to interact with her at an emotional level. So she has found exactly what she needs. She'll be your patient for a long time, Stephen."

In continued reflection Stephen talked about how he marveled at Jalee's remarkable accomplishments. Here she was, a Native American with a high school education who, based on her intelligence and talents, her determination and her will, had achieved what anyone knowing her would consider a remarkably successful life. He was not surprised if some of the people she knew felt fortunate to know her. In a way it was sad that Jalee seemed to have no appreciation of her own gifts or the esteem she had in others eyes. Or perhaps that lack of self-view was her greatest gift: she had pride in her heritage but an absence of conscious need for personal admiration from others. He felt certain her relationship with the Great Spirit breathed meaning into her life.

Doctor Moke's next meeting with Jalee was mostly about music. The juke box was installed shortly after her last visit. The café patrons were pleased with the music background but not with Jalee's choice of classical music. They were frank in response to her questioning and she had questioned almost all of them. The consensus favored what one might call 'cowboy western' music. In searching for a change of music she bought some Willey Nelson and Johnny Cash records which won unanimous approval.

As Jalee finished telling Doctor Moke about the success of the juke box, she smiled and added the comment, "I have a secret." This was the first time Moke had a glimpse of a more open and freer side of Jalee. The comment sounded like a tease, a "try to guess the answer." He was surprised by the almost child-like attitude. She continued, "I went to the café one evening after telling John I wanted to do some tidying. When I got there I pulled down the shades, left the lights off and got out my saxophone from its hiding place. I turned on the juke box and accompanied the music on my sax. It was glorious. I played and played until I could hardly breathe. I was tempted to go outside and play to the stars."

Jalee's enthusiasm and delight were obvious. Doctor Moke commented, "An audience would surely have appreciated it. You should try it on your customers one day; only they would probably stop eating to listen and not finish their lunch. Did they have Pow Wows when you were a young girl on the reservation? And if they occurred, did you ever dance in one?"

Jalee responded, "Oh, yes, they had them. I was too young to dance in them, but my father danced and played the flute with other flute players, drummers and dancers. I especially liked the Pow Wow on the night of a new moon. The stars were always brighter and seemed to shine and dance with the music. Those happy times returned to me that night at the café as a gift from the Great Spirit."

Moke commented, "It's too bad you couldn't have shared that evening with John or someone you know."

Jalee said, "I shared it with the stars and with my father. Now I shared it with you and that will keep it fresh in my mind for many moons and many starry nights. And my time is finished. Should I return in two weeks?"

"Yes, of course," Moke replied, "And thank you for sharing your night of music. I'm sure your father must have been listening. I'll see you in two weeks."

Jalee continued regular visits at two week intervals for another six months. Then one day she asked if she could come less frequently, perhaps once a month with an occasional visit in between if she was "having difficulty." She gave no explanation of what "difficulty" meant and Moke decided not to ask. They had reached a point where the nuances of their relationship had become more significant. Moke felt his "need to know" as a therapist was partially replaced by some process in his mind that was subconsciously filling in the blanks. He was aware (or at least believed) the same process was on occasion happening in Jalee's mind. He didn't believe in mental telepathy as such, but this subtle process kept nudging his mind to believe they had some unusual transfer of thoughts.

In response to Jalee's request Doctor Moke replied, "Of course, we can make the change. How would it be if I gave you an appointment every four weeks at this usual time? You can call during the four-week interval and request an additional visit if you wish. If you call, I will arrange an appointment at the earliest time available. I'm aware of your hours at the café so I will give you the first appointment available outside of those hours. To schedule or change appointments just call my answering service. The number is on my office card. The answering service will give me the message and I will return your call as soon as I'm available." As she was leaving, Doctor Moke gave her another of his cards with the date of the next interview in four weeks.

During the visit four weeks later Moke decided he would broach a subject they both had ignored. He thought it might be an area which would expand Jalee's world in a significant and positive way. After some preliminary exchanges bringing Moke up to the latest in café stories, he opened the topic saying, "Jalee, have you ever thought of trying to get in touch with your daughter? Do you know where she is? Do you know anything about her present life? Have you ever seen her since your grandfather's funeral?"

Jalee replied, "The last time I saw her was at the funeral. She barely spoke to me and she left abruptly once the service was over. She may still be living in the house where grandfather lived. I doubt if he made any legal arrangements about his property. It wasn't our custom. Susan probably stayed there unless she couldn't pay the taxes. I feel sure she is not destitute. She's probably working somewhere in Spokane. I've never seen her on the streets but then I rarely go to Spokane. I have no need or desire to see her."

Moke pressed her a little, "Aren't you a bit curious about what her life is like? Suppose she has children? Would you be interested if you had grandchildren? After all they would be your descendants, part of your lineage."

Jalee responded softly, "I'll think about it." Then she went on, "John made a fenced area for my dogs about a week ago. They were getting rather numerous and I was keeping them all on leashes. People know I have them and occasionally someone will show up looking for their dog. I'm always happy to return a dog to its owner. The reunion makes me think of the time when I will return to my owner just as the dogs will all return someday to the One who will be kind to them forever. The kennel seemed like a gift from John although he didn't even mention it to me. He just built it. He is really a kind man even though he doesn't like dogs. As I say that, I wonder if it may be the same with me. He's kind to me but perhaps he doesn't like me."

Doctor Moke almost interrupted in his desire to reassure Jalee. "John was clearly concerned about your welfare when you got the summons from the policeman and he continued to show his support and attention throughout that time. From what you say, John has shared important parts of your life perhaps not directly but indirectly. For example, some decisions about the café and about the house you bought and now rent. You discussed and shared some of those decisions with him. He probably shares more of your life than you share of his at the railroad station."

Jalee responded, "That's true. And that's about all we have in common. As I mentioned before, I read a lot and listen to music and take care of my strays. John spends time puttering around in his shop. He's a Mason and attends their meetings regularly. On rare occasions he plays poker with friends from work. He attends his church on Sunday. He has asked me if I'd like to go to church with him. But I told him my church is just outside my kitchen door. I just step out and night or day commune with the Great Spirit."

Doctor Moke continued trying to expand Jalee's view of her marriage. "Some people don't express emotions easily, especially men. They sometimes act like they're ashamed of emotions or see them as a weakness. They will do nice things for someone else because they genuinely care for that person. But you might never hear them express that caring in words. After just meeting John a couple of times I would guess he might be one of those people." In his mind Doctor Moke doubted there had ever been any deep emotional or physical intimacy in the marriage. At the same time it appeared to be an unwavering union and one which provided a stabilizing relationship for both of them. In the long run it was probably more fulfilling for John than for Jalee. She looked very attentive as he made the comments about John.

Then she moved on and talked about one of her new dogs, one that only let her approach when she spoke soothingly and moved slowly. She said the dog was probably beaten by the prior owner. The dog found a caring refuge with Jalee. Was Jalee consciously making a comparison with her own life? Moke wondered if she was thinking of her own abused past and the refuge she found with John. Perhaps John found Jalee rather distant and guarded toward him because of her past. During Jalee's therapy sessions Moke believed she often made connections like these but without need for his commenting. He had the impression her mind actively pursued many of these loose threads of her life.

Doctor Moke let his personal interest pose his question, "You mention the new dog you've found, a dog you suspect had been beaten. How do you establish a relationship with such a dog?"

Jalee responded, "I move slowly and calmly and before I reach out my hand I talk to the dog. You have to talk to an animal for them to know you. It's the same with horses and birds. But that's not surprising. We must talk to the Great Spirit to be known. Silence doesn't breathe or live or even stir the air. Words bridge those who are separate."

Something occurred two weeks later which was a surprise to Doctor Moke. One day he called his answering service during the few minutes he had between patients. In those days the answering service involved an actual person answering the call and taking a message. The person at the service told Moke there was a call from the Elm area but the caller hung up when she answered. Moke immediately decided, no *knew,* Jalee had called. He called Jalee's number. She answered the phone, said nothing about having called, but asked him for an appointment. He gave her a four o'clock the following Tuesday. After the call was completed it amused him to reflect on Jalee's use of the telephone almost as a primitive horn or drum to communicate. The Native Americans were adept at using hand signals within sight of each other (as our police and military do). But when there was a distance they used horns or drumming sounds to signal, sounds which could not be interpreted or interrupted by their enemies (of which there were many). Jalee, perhaps instinctively, used the answering service like her ancestors used drums. This way of contact continued throughout the time of Jalee's care.

Doctor Moke was never certain of the reason for this appointment or any of the other "extra appointments" Jalee requested. It was an unspoken understanding they had. She could ask for the appointment but she need not "discuss the reason or explain." During this visit Jalee mentioned she had seen her daughter, Susan, who brought her four-year-old son to their meeting. Susan was living in the grandfather's house with her son and her Caucasian husband. She named her son Joseph after his maternal great-grandfather.

Doctor Moke asked Jalee how the meeting went because she only volunteered it had occurred. Her reply was rather brief, "It was nice to see Susan again but I doubt there will be any further contact. She has adopted Caucasian ways. She is self-centered and focused on fashion and the 'latest' of everything. She works in a Spokane department store and apparently spends a lot of time with friends from the store. Her husband works in a near-by service station. Her son is rather poorly behaved for a four-year-old. We have little in common. But thank you for encouraging me to meet with her. I'm glad I did. It was one of those things I've been avoiding in life."

Doctor Moke said, "I'm sorry it was not a more pleasant and enriching meeting for you. Maybe it will help you close the book on that part of your life which I'm sure has many unpleasant memories for you."

Jalee sat quietly for a minute or so before responding, "The happy memories are still alive and so real they chase away the shadows from the past. The wind whispers and the stars shine reminding me of the good times when my father was alive and those times return to me."

The rest of the session seemed to wander through the day-to-day of Jalee's life. At the end of the meeting she simply said she would return for her usual appointment in another two weeks. Doctor Moke decided Jalee made this appointment because she wanted to tell him about her daughter's visit. Perhaps the visit was more meaningful than she had acknowledged.

When Moke went to the waiting room he found a large book of famous artists: glossy pictures beautifully bound and displayed. Inside the front cover was the check for the visit. This was the beginning of a pattern for Jalee. Every two or three visits there would be a similar book of famous artists or views of famous places (towns or nature scenes). Of course, Jalee was gone by the time he picked up the book. At the time of her next visit it never seemed appropriate for him to mention the book Jalee left after the previous visit. To mention the book (left after the prior session) would be a distraction from the session which was beginning. He decided the books could not be mixed into the material of treatment work.

His decision was violated after their session prior to Christmas. On that occasion Jalee left an imported limited-edition Swiss music box, an obviously expensive gift. When Jalee came for her visit after Christmas,

Doctor Moke began the visit with a, "Thank you-----," Jalee held up her hand, "There is no need. The world is the only gift that needs a reply of gratitude. Let me tell you about one of the dogs" and she went on with her story.

After six or seven additional monthly visits, Jalee proposed she continue appointments but not on a regular schedule. She would call the answering service and plan to take the next available appointment in keeping with her work schedule. Doctor Moke was agreeable so the arrangement was made. Jalee's calls to the answering service continued as before. A call, a hang-up, Moke informed of a call from the Elm exchange, his call to Jalee. The drums beat on and the messages got through.

Jalee continued seeing Doctor Moke for another two years with this pattern of scattered appointments. He was tempted to ask her why she never left a message with the answering service. He decided it might be better not to ask. Sometimes he wondered if Jalee thought the operator at the answering service would recognize her voice (unlikely if they never heard it before), or they might check the number she would give them and know it was the Jalee café or her residence. Was Jalee concerned someone might know she was seeing a psychiatrist and make a judgement about it or gossip about it? Was she safeguarding the privacy that seemed so sacred to her? Was it personal or was it tribal or was it both? He came to the conclusion that this bond between them was more meaningful that the usual patient-doctor relationship. There was a revered connection which should not be intruded upon by "the knowing" of others.

Whatever the barrier was that kept him from expressing his gratitude for the books and the music box; it also prevented him from changing his fees for Jalee. When he first saw Jalee he was relatively new in the area. Consequently, his initial fee was based on his previous charges and was considerably less than the average fee in this area. During his years of practice in Spokane he became more aware of the standard fees in the locale and so he increased his own fees to be within the same range. As a result, Jalee's fee should be nearly double what he charged when she first became his patient. Doctor Moke could not bring himself to increase Jalee's fee. He questioned his reasoning. He saw their relationship as a special agreement they made and to change the fee would violate their relationship, this imaginary pact. His final conclusion was that he could not explain and need not explain the mystery and meaning of his own behavior.

Moke frequently considered going for lunch at the Jalee café, a short drive from the office. It wasn't just professional ethics that marked the boundary between him and Jalee. There was an unworldly element, a revered bond unique in his professional experience. Jalee's use of words and phrases revealed a certain peace that accompanied her presence in his office and reflected a spiritual component. There was never a hint of anger or revenge or criticism in her words. There was pain, but there was peace. There was hurt, but there was healing. There was fear, but there was bravery. Lunch at the Jalee Café would certainly violate their relationship.

During one of her appointments Jalee told Doctor Moke how John recently modified a small room in the house to be her library. He built shelves for her books. He asked Jalee to choose the furniture. As she looked around the office, she said, "I wanted to make it look like this room." She pointed to a lamp on a lamp-stand in the corner. The lamp had a stained glass half-globe with glass dangles hanging from the edge of the globe. "I tried to find a lamp like yours but couldn't come even close to matching it. That lamp is my beacon, my life-saving light; when I'm lonely or sad or out of sorts I think about that lamp. It calms me and gives me courage."

There was no doubt or hesitation in her comment. It was a simple statement with a significant meaning. Moke realized his office was a haven for Jalee Clark, a place of peace and contemplation even from a distance. It turned out that her comment was fortuitous for Moke and for Jalee.

After her next visit Jalee left a small, leather bound, blank-page book with a note inside on a small slip of paper. On the note: "Always I had planned to fill this book with poetry and music, then hide it carefully away with the saxophone for someone to find years from now and wonder. It isn't going to happen. Your decorator made this room as lovely as a symphony so she can probably fill this with the music of words. Someone should write in it. Books should not be wasted." The book was obviously meant for his wife. That evening he gave the book to Ann and simply said, "From Jalee."

It was several months after Jalee's comment about the lamp when Stephen and Ann began to talk of moving again. A small, about to be established, psychiatric hospital in Philadelphia contacted Stephen with an invitation to apply for the position of Hospital Administrator. The new hospital, Harvey Institute, was to have an inpatient and outpatient program exclusively for professional religious personnel needing mental health care.

There were several reasons why the offer appealed to both of them. Ann was born in Philadelphia and grew up in the K and A (Kensington and Allegany) area. A favorite aunt of hers plus some cousins and old friends were still living in the city. She had many pleasant memories of her early life there and she was particularly fond of her Aunt Edith. Her parents and Ann moved to New Jersey when Ann was fifteen.

Doctor Moke did his three-year psychiatric residency program in Philadelphia and met Ann there when she was back for a lengthy visit with her Aunt Edith. The city was familiar to both of them. Their interest grew as they discussed the invitation Stephen received. They finally decided it would be a good idea to go back, visit Aunt Edith, look around, get information on housing prices; and Stephen would set up an interview at the Harvey Institute.

It was a few weeks before Doctor Moke could clear his schedule for the week's trip. As he considered the possibility of leaving the Spokane area he knew he would undoubtedly have his own personal and professional regrets and qualms about leaving his patients. A move was always a struggle for him. In leaving he felt like he was abandoning his patients. He tried to make the transition as easy as possible for them. He would give them two months' notice and recommend two or three other practitioners whom they might find compatible for their needs. As he considered the possibility of making this change, Jalee's name came to mind. What would happen to Jalee? He suspected even the décor of his office was perhaps almost as significant for her as he was. Their relationship was certainly unique. If he referred her to someone how could he describe their relationship or the intricate road they travelled to get there? He couldn't even explain it to himself. There were spiritual components; there was communication half-spoken but fully understood; and there were tinges of thought that somehow traveled between them. He knew he couldn't describe their relationship to another therapist. He could only hope Jalee might find another person in her life with whom she would feel comfortable spending time and talking about happenings and feelings she experienced.

Stephen and Ann made their scheduled trip to Philadelphia on a Monday. They stayed at a Ramada Inn close to the Harvey Institute. On Tuesday they visited Aunt Edith and took her to lunch. Stephen's interview with George Gomey, Acting Director of the Institute, was scheduled for Wednesday. Stephen asked Ann to accompany him to the interview because he valued her observations.

The interview went well. Gomey guaranteed Stephen considerable autonomy and left no doubt he would be captain of the ship once it was launched. Establishing the Institute was based on their belief that "religion professionals" (as they chose to call them) faced unusual situations and challenges. They hypothesized that religion professionals often feel awkward and uncomfortable in seeking therapy because the laity might misconstrue or be scandalized by their need for treatment.

As the lengthy interview came to a close, George Gomey commented, "This is the age of ecumenism and all religion professionals share common problems, experiences and emotional issues. This facility will bring them together and enhance this sharing of communality.

"We are recruiting a group of mental health professionals who will bring special skills to this work. Recommendations from several individuals who worked with you and for you, Doctor Moke, made us decide to hire you, if you'll take the job."

Doctor Moke said, "This has all been very interesting. Thank you. Your Harvey Institute is intriguing, a fascinating and attractive idea. Ann and I will talk it over and let you known by Wednesday of next week or possibly earlier. You haven't mentioned a salary."

George Gomey gave Moke a figure which was a few thousand more than Stephen had expected. Stephen and Ann said goodbye to George and left. They spent the next two days looking at houses for sale, houses mostly in the area not far from the Harvey facility. They found a couple of good possibilities in a pleasant neighborhood about a mile from the Harvey Institute. They spent time on Friday afternoon with Aunt Edith and a couple of Ann's friends from the past.

They returned to Spokane Saturday morning. During the trip home they talked very little about a possible move to Philadelphia. This was characteristic of their relationship. Each went through their own process of reviewing and evaluating the information they had obtained. A few hours after they arrived home, Ann asked Stephen, "Do you think you're ready to discuss our future or do you want more time?"

Stephen replied, "I'm ready if you are. I'm ready to talk but not sure I'm ready to decide. Do you want to tell me your thoughts about the possibility of making the move?"

Ann said, "I'll give it a try. First of all, I have mixed feelings about leaving Spokane. I like being in the West and we've had a good life here. We also have some good friends but we've left good friends before, and we know people in Philly with whom we'll undoubtedly be friends if we move there. Being in Philly and thinking of the possibility of living there highlighted something that's been floating around in the back of my mind for some time. I think I'd like to start going to church again. I was quite involved in the Catholic Church I attended in Philly until I left there when I was fifteen.

"I know all I've said hasn't even referred to the key issue, namely the job. That's really the critical part so it's important to know where you are with the Harvey haven. I think of it as a sort of haven, a place to retreat to when health professionals have had all they can take. A few of my thoughts. There's a risk in George Gomey's venture. It could be a complete failure. But I'm intrigued by the facility he's planning. I don't know if you would agree but I see religion professionals as needing a treatment facility designed for them in their unusual life work. How do you feel about it all, Stephen?"

Stephen began in his usual methodical way. "I have several concerns. Probably my most immediate concern is abandoning my patients. I know 'abandoning' is an exaggeration, but it is the issue that initially comes to mind. I agree with your feelings about leaving Spokane and the West. The 'friend issue' probably plays a more important part for you than it does for me. Your mention of 'a return to church' could occur here as well as in Philadelphia. Perhaps we should give some thought to that whether we move or not.

"As you say, the most important issue is the risk in Gomey's narrowly specialized psychiatric facility. It is an attractive concept. I believe religion professionals do have a difficult role in life. Their work combines the spiritual and the emotional simultaneously in their response to the needs and lives of those they serve. I have often wondered if the concurrent involvement in both areas creates conflict and stress. I sometimes have a difficult time clearly sorting out the two issues in my own work.

"On the one hand, the religion professional is doing spiritual guidance and emotional counseling at the same time. They are trained in spiritual guidance. *That* is what they're all about. But emotional factors are typically involved. There is no clear line between the spiritual and the emotional. What's the toll on their personal lives?"

Ann smiled and said, "Apparently you've been giving this more thought than I realized. I've been wondering why you've been so quiet. Remember our agreement: better to talk it over together than to mull it over alone. Obviously, you're more than just interested in the Harvey Institute."

During the evening Stephen and Ann walked a half-mile to a favorite restaurant for dinner. As they walked home they continued their discussion. Before they retired for the night, they agreed Stephen would take the job and they would plan to leave within the next two or three months. In the morning they would write down the things to be done to begin their preparation. Getting ready for bed, Ann said, "Since tomorrow is Sunday and we'll be starting a new future, let's go to Mass at St. Al's and ask a blessing on our venture." Stephen agreed and turned out the light.

The next day they went to the ten a.m. Mass at St. Aloysius parish. After being absent so many years it still felt familiar to be in a Catholic Church again. On their return home they agreed to continue regular Sunday Mass attendance.

Then they took up the task of writing down what each one would take care of in anticipation of the move to Philadelphia. They looked at the information they had gathered on three different homes for sale and discussed the pros and cons of each. They decided they had enough information on the one house they chose without seeing it again. Ann would deal with the realtor by phone on Monday. Ann would also make appointments with two or three movers and get a price from each. Stephen would deal with the company who held his office rental contract. He would also compose a letter for each of his patients notifying them of his departure. The letter needed to be individualized so he could include names of two or three colleagues whom he considered a good match for each patient.

When he came to Jalee's letter, he didn't know what to do, whom to recommend. He asked Ann for a suggestion, but she offered no help other than to say, "That's a tough one. I suggest you trust the Great Spirit." Stephen finally decided to recommend Jalee ask Doctor Mansfield if and when she felt the need to continue treatment. He would also write a brief note to Doctor Mansfield and give him his own thinking: first, that Jalee would probably not be comfortable with another therapist and second, that Doctor Moke didn't feel she needed to continue in treatment at least at the present time. He would let Mansfield know but he wouldn't personally tell Jalee either of these things because he was concerned she might interpret it as rejection or that Moke felt he had been wasting his time to meet with her.

So his plan was not to send Jalee a letter but to tell her about his leaving during her next visit. Jalee called within the week and asked for an appointment. He had notified her that he would be away for a week so he was not surprised by her call. Perhaps she needed reassurance he had returned. He gave her a four o'clock the following week.

On the day of Jalee's appointment Doctor Moke was distracted during his time with other patients. It annoyed him because it was highly unusual. Each patient had a separate story and the appointment time should be totally dedicated to that particular story. His mind kept wandering to Jalee and concern for her reaction.

His appointment with Jalee began as usual. She seemed in good spirits and said she was glad he was back. She began talking about how well the new kennel was working out for the dogs and how glad she was John built it. She continued with news of the café. They were about twenty minutes into the interview when Doctor Moke had the opportunity to say, "I'm afraid I have some bad news, Jalee. I will be closing my office in about two months. My wife and I are moving to . . ."

It wasn't a shriek that came from Jalee. It was a loud cry that never seemed to leave her throat but somehow filled the air as Jalee stood, turned away and walked out of the office carefully closing the door. Doctor Moke had an impulse to run after her and bring her back. But he sat stunned by what happened. Her response: was it a battle cry or the howl of a wounded animal? It was almost frightening to hear. He expected Jalee might be or at least appear to be stoic over his leaving. He speculated she might experience rage and be accusatory over another 'white man's' abuse or abandonment. He thought "perhaps that's what her reaction did say."

Then he realized he was feeling abandoned by Jalee and he began to wonder how he would get to see her again before he left Spokane. He sat there feeling desperately in need of a kinder farewell for the two of them or at least for himself. He began talking out loud. Will she call? Will she make another appointment? If she doesn't contact me, should I go to the Jalee café to see her? Or to her house? It sounds rather foolish, a psychiatrist stalking his former patient to say goodbye to her. But what can I do? I need to get this to a better level before I ever leave Spokane." He suddenly realized he was talking out loud. Jalee was the last patient of the day. He was glad for that. He couldn't face another patient with this cluttered mind.

He tried to find relief as he walked out of his office and locked the door, but he couldn't lock his thoughts inside. He took them home and followed the pattern he and Ann had agreed on, "discuss the burdens of the day before spending their evening together." It was difficult to tell, but more difficult not to tell, Jalee's reaction to his announcement of departure.

Ann responded with her usual gentleness. "It really should have been no great surprise to you, sweetheart. Jalee is deeply attached to you as I expected she would be. I once suggested that would occur. And you have grown attached to her; otherwise today's behavior would not be so traumatic for you. At this point I'm afraid you can only wait for Jalee to heal her loss if she can. From what you've told me she has not been good at healing losses; there was her maternal grandfather, her first husband, her daughter and probably a few others you've heard about. I would guess it will take her some time to come to an understanding of your departure and that your life has its own demands and concerns.

"We have almost two months before we leave. If you have heard nothing after several weeks, you could try calling her. I assume you've thought of going to the café or to her home. I think she might well find such a visit invasive. This woman has a tribal sense of boundaries: territorial, spiritual and personal."

Stephen felt relieved to be able to talk about it all. He agreed he would just have to wait and perhaps Jalee would contact him. If he didn't hear from her in three or four weeks he would call her.

It was exactly four weeks later that he picked up the phone at four in the afternoon, Jalee's usual appointment day and time. He dialed hoping she would answer and afraid she might not. The call was answered with, "Hello, is this the doctor calling? This is Jalee." Was it the four o'clock time of the call or was it some native intuition? Moke noted she didn't say the doctor's name out of her privacy need.

He responded, "Yes, Jalee, it's doctor Moke. I have called to ask you to visit my office once more. I would like the opportunity to explain to you why I am leaving the area and tell you how troubled I am that I will no longer be available for our visits. It is important for me and possibly for you to allow me to summarize your care and to say a peace-filled goodbye. Would you be kind enough to come to the office once more?"

Jalee replied, "Yes, I will come another time. The Great Spirit blesses those who seek peace. May I come at this time next week?"

"Yes, that will be fine. Thank you for your generous response, Jalee. I will look forward to the visit." Doctor Moke was greatly relieved with the result of his call. A bit of euphoria as he thought, "If I had a saxophone; I'd play it."

Of course, when he got home he reported the conversation to Ann. She could see his relief as he walked in the door. It was a cause to celebrate with a glass of wine before dinner. As they were talking after dinner, Stephen told Ann he would like to give Jalee one of the lamps in the office. He described the lamp and said Jalee had once referred to the lamp as a beacon in her life when she was troubled. Ann responded, "I think that's a great idea. She will be pleased but you should be prepared for her to reject it. My guess is you will not be able to persuade her to accept it."

The week passed and Doctor Moke was prepared for Jalee's appointment.

Since the Mokes were preparing to move, there were boxes of all sizes and shapes to choose from. He found a sturdy cardboard box big enough for the lamp and a roll of packing paper to pack around it. His heart was set on Jalee taking the lamp.

Moke was feeling uneasy when Jalee arrived. They went through their simple greetings. Jalee appeared to be at ease and her manner reassured him. He began, "How are things going since I last saw you?"

Jalee responded, "I do have a funny story I've been wanting to tell you. It happened last week. One evening I baked four cherry pies and had them in the car the following morning as I drove to the café. I was going about sixty on the highway when a car came out from a side road ahead of me. I slammed on the brakes but I was too close and hit the other car. There was little damage to my car but a lot of damage to the other car. I thanked the Great Spirit no one was injured. You would have laughed if you'd seen the result. I was covered with cherry pie. It was all over me and the inside of my car. No one in the café had cherry pie for lunch that day. I could hardly get clear of the cherries by lunch time.

Moke was laughing when he responded, "It must have been quite a sight. How could you ever get it cleaned up by lunch time? It is a blessing there were no injuries."

Jalee said she just got herself ready by lunch time and cleaned the car later in the evening. She continued with a few additional comments about the reaction of others to the incident.

Then Doctor Moke brought up the reason for their meeting. "Thank you for coming today, Jalee. I was hoping for an opportunity to meet with you again. I wanted to try to help you understand why my wife and I are leaving Spokane. My wife is from Philadelphia and I did some of my studies there. My wife's favorite aunt is living there as well as several other relatives and friends from the past. I've been offered a position as a director of an unusual psychiatric clinic, a clinic to care for the emotional problems of all the men and women who serve as ministers for the Great Spirit. This clinic will offer specialized treatment for this select group of the Great Spirit's workers and I believe it will be a privilege to assist in their care.

"I will give you the address of our home in Philadelphia and I encourage you to write to me if you would like to let me know how you are or if you have something special you would like to tell me or ask me. If you should ever be in the Philadelphia area, I hope you will let me know and come visit us." Moke knew a visit would never occur and that a letter was highly unlikely and he knew Jalee knew it too. The Native American adage: "Whether you walk it or not, it's a kindly trail that has a friend at the other end." Moke gave her his office card with the Philadelphia address written on the back. Actually it was quite unprofessional for Moke to be talking about writing to or visiting with a former patient. He knew Jalee was more to him than just being a patient.

Doctor Moke then summarized their meetings and reminded Jalee of the work she did and the progress she made. He talked about her as a peace-loving woman who was kind and caring for others, a friend and guardian of the Great Spirit's creation. He reminded her how she benefitted from her relationship with the sky and all it holds of stars and the two great lights. He spoke of her care and companionship with the Spirit's earth creatures. He mentioned that as she deepened her meditative times she found they absorbed her angry, anxious and sad feelings. Doctor Moke continued, "Your relationship with the heavens and all they reveal and your companionship with animals and birds, all this brings meaning and strength and peace to a lonely world."

Doctor Moke reassured Jalee saying he believed she had benefited from their meetings and she had established greater inner strength and better understanding of the challenges of life. He said, "if later on you feel a need to talk to a psychiatrist you should contact Doctor Mansfield and ask whom he would recommend."

Doctor Moke continued, "And today I want to give you something from the office which you once described as a beacon, a light to brighten the dark of sadness and anger you sometimes feel. I would be honored if you would accept the lamp you looked at so many times during these many months and keep it as a reminder of the blessed meetings we have shared."

Jalee had tears as she smiled and shook her head saying, "You were the gift and I am grateful. Our native idea of existence is that every person has a purpose. I have had time to reflect on that reality of life. Your purpose is calling you to Philadelphia. Yes, we have talked many times and I have learned. When I talk to the animals and the birds they talk to me and we know each other. You and I know each other. It is a blessing that will go on and on. I will talk to you when you are gone, as I talk to my father. And I will hear you answer. Life continues to teach me so I must learn. Loneliness is a blessing when it brings back thoughts of a good friend.

"The lamp belongs in your office. It was chosen by your wife and contains her care and wisdom."

Doctor Moke was prepared for Jalee's comment. "I discussed this decision with my wife. I told her I had a patient who remarked about the lamp as you have. I said I was planning to give that patient the lamp as a token of peace and friendship. My wife strongly agreed and said she would be pleased to have the lamp in the hands of a former patient who occupied a memorable place in my work and in my life. So my wife has given her consent and will be delighted by the arrangement.

"Now I'll ask you just to remain in your chair a short time. I have brought a box for the lamp and paper to wrap around it. It will only take me a minute or two to get it ready."

Moke completed the packing and brought the box toward Jalee. As he approached, Jalee stood and reached out to take it. There were tears in her eyes as she embraced the box and turned to leave. Moke walked to open the office door and then walked through the waiting room to open the door to the hall.

There were no words, only tears as Jalee left with the shared lamp, the shared affection, and shared beliefs in the Great Spirit who linked their lives for a time, time that will continue in the stars, the wind, and the mysteries of life.

Doctor Moke closed his psychiatric practice the end of that week; so there were many more goodbyes, significant but less moving sentimentally or spiritually. The following week the movers picked up the office furniture and then came for the house furniture and belongings. Ann and Stephen each drove a car on the long trip to Philadelphia.

After arrival in Philadelphia there was only a week before Stephen took over as Director of the Harvey Institute. The majority of staff was already hired and in place. George Gomey, who planned it all, was going to take the Business Manager position. He had prepared a grand opening with extensive advertising.

A nationally known Rabbi, a local Catholic Bishop, and a female Episcopal pastor spoke briefly at the opening ceremony on a Friday afternoon. Thirty-three local pastors attended plus fourteen members of the mental health professions. Each of the speakers praised the institution for recognizing their special work on the sacred bridge between the mundane and the spiritual, between sanity and sanctity (as one of them said.) Each asked God's blessing on this novel facility. Mr. Gomey introduced Doctor Moke who spoke briefly to the assembly and later met briefly with the institute staff.

Three months later Stephen and Ann were still getting settled in their new home. It was on an acre and a half lot, a two story three-bedroom house with large rooms on the first floor, a two car garage and full finished basement. They brought Ann's favorite aunt over to show her the house and to convince her they really were going to live in Philadelphia.

Then one day a letter came to their house addressed to Doctor Stephen Moke. The return address was a Rural Route Box Number in Elm, Washington. Ann felt sure it must be from Jalee. When Stephen got home that evening he immediately opened the letter. It was from John Clark and read as follows:

Dear Doctor Moke,

I regret the need to write this letter and to have to tell you Jalee is dead. After dinner one evening she went to feed the dogs and spend her usual thirty or forty minutes talking to them. An hour and a half passed and I decided to see if everything was alright in the kennel. I found Jalee lying dead on the ground. All the kennel dogs were lying around her as if they were in mourning.

I called the police and told them how I found Jalee. They sent a car and an ambulance and after checking the situation they removed her body. One of the officers later called me and said the coroner decided Jalee died of a heart attack.

I decided to write to you because Jalee often mentioned you. In addition, there was a lamp with a round half-globe that seemed almost sacred to her. In speaking of it she once referred to your office. I'm wondering if the lamp is familiar to you and would you like to have me send it to you? Please, let me know if you would like to have the lamp.

Finally, perhaps you are a religious man and if you are, would you ask the God you believe in to grant Jalee peace and happiness; something I'm not sure I was ever successful at doing.

Sincerely,
(Signed) John Clark

Ann reached for Stephen's hand and said, "Come and sit with me for a while. I know how you loved Jalee, how dear she was to you. Yes, Stephen, let the tears come; they'll ease the loss of this brave Native American woman, a loss to many but perhaps most deeply to you. Undoubtedly you knew the depth of her need to be with the Great Spirit. Now she is there and with the father who communicated with her through the years. I wouldn't be surprised if you hear her talking silently to you one day."

Stephen continued to dry his eyes as Ann held him in her arms and tried to comfort him. He spoke, "Thank you, my love, for being so understanding. I felt a bond with Jalee from the first day I saw her. Her stature was so striking. It spoke of a healthy pride in who she was. My affection had nothing to do with earthly love. It was of another place, another world. It just occurred to me, I'm glad we've returned to practicing our faith. It will make contact with Jalee more natural and more likely."

A week later the box arrived with the office lamp. The lamp was given a special place in the Moke living room and was always referred to as *Jalee's lamp*. It became a symbol of many things for Ann and Stephen: avoidance of racial and religious prejudice, respect for all especially the demeaned, the outcast, an inner sense of a spirit realm, a feeling of intimacy with loved ones who communicate in the drum beat of our heart. With a low watt bulb, the lamp was constantly alight, a ray from a caring friend.